To: Michelle Austin

Situations

Love to you!

101

An Up-Close Focus on Relationship Dramas

The best of Good Times

Situations

101

An Up-Close Focus
on
Relationship Dramas

Bern Nadette Stanis

Worthingham Publishing

Published by:
Worthingham Publishing
8306 Wilshire Blvd. Suite 303
Beverly Hills, CA 90211

In conjunction with:
Old Mountain Press, Inc.
2542 S. Edgewater Dr.
Fayetteville, NC 28303

www.oldmountainpress.com

Copyright © 2005 Bern Nadette Stanis
Interior text design by Tom Davis
Edited by Sam Zahran
ISBN: 978-0-9770361-0-3
Library of Congress Control Number: 2006923133

Situations 101 An Up-Close Focus on Relationship Dramas.

First Edition
Printed and bound in the United States of America by Sumi Printing & Binding
www.getsumi.com • 310-769-1600
1 2 3 4 5 6 7 8 9 10

Dedication

With All My Love

To My Family

Everywhere

And

You Know Who

You Are

Foreword

*S*ituations 101 is a book that I have created about different situations in relationships. I wrote them in the hope that maybe you can relate to a few of them. You may even find some of these situations in your own life. But if not, believe me; you will still find it to be interesting reading.

I welcome communicating with others about issues concerning relationships, issues such as self-esteem, whether one is in or out of a relationship at the time, and having confidence to continue on the path to accomplish your goal of finding that special person in your life, even when it looks like he or she is nowhere in sight.

If you would like to discuss any of these situations, or if you have other related relationship issues that you care to discuss, I will be available at various times for discussion at:

Goodtimesthelma@aol.com
www.thelmaofgoodtimes.com

Disclaimer: The situations in this book are not all mine, however all of these situations are real and have happened to someone. I took 101 of these situations and created scenarios around them and my responses to them. These scenarios bring focus to what is going on in some relationships today. I only hope that after reading them, they will inspire in you a determination to keep your own relationships healthy.

Table of Contents

Situations:

Situation

1 Love Is the Only Thing That Lasts

We met when he came to my city to work for a few months. Right after his assignment, he went back to his hometown. He had been married before and divorced and had two small children. His life was complicated, and I was single with no children and ready for a man like him. But as time went on, I realized that our lives were going in different directions and we were not going to be together.

This devastated me at the time, but our love never died. We stayed in contact with each other. In our way we stayed close.

It's been more than 10 years ago, and now we both want to be together. It is very frightening for me, and he has told me it is frightening for him too. But we want to give this a try.

We really don't have anything in common but our love for each other. Do you think we can finally have the love we've always dreamed of?

My grandmother once told me that love is the only thing that lasts. Do you believe love conquers all?

Response:

This sounds like it could be the perfect fairy tale ending. I know there has been a lot of living in his life that did not include you and vice versa. But it does seem like there is a real love between the two of you. The two of you will have to find out about this love that you have for each other. This will happen after the two of you are together and living an everyday life instead of one that is not together every day.

To answer your question, do I believe love conquers all, well, I hate to be a wet blanket, but I don't believe love conquers all! I believe there is so much more to it than that. There are a lot of factors involved when you are talking about two people being together, even if their love for one another is strong. To have major factors already in place when two people meet is certainly a lot to consider. The two of you fell in love like couples do but never had the chance to develop the love. But I do believe all things are in the right timing.

Maybe 10 years ago it just wasn't the timing for this relationship. If the two of you had pursued it at that time, it is possible that the interference of the other things in both of your lives would have choked out the love that remains, for the two of you today.

Although I am a believer that love does not conquer all, I will agree with your grandmother that love lasts forever. I say this because there are classic love stories about people who fell in love when they were young and were not together in life but at the end of their lives they called for that loved one. Or at the end of their lives they would say that they never stopped loving that one certain person. So, yes, I believe love is the one and only thing that lasts forever.

Even though you have known each other many years, it is as if the two of you are starting a new relationship. Treat it as such because this is the only way to give your love a fair chance. Just see where it goes, and because the love between the two of you is still there and very strong, I do believe this love will live on. The two of you may even go down in history as the perfect fairytale couple. Good luck to the both of you, and may you both live happily and lovingly ever after, with one another.

Situation

2 Friction Started When I Called My Man's Friend

A male friend of mine whom I have been seeing for two years now has moved away. He said it is for his business. We both are very busy all the time, so we had a good schedule of seeing each other. We would see each other once a week, and this was perfect for the two of us. Lately I have been feeling he has been pushing me away.

There are times when he and I would get into an argument, and the things he would say would cause distance between us. But it was the last argument we had that really went off the hook. This time he pushed me too far. He called me some names and degraded me. I was so upset by this that I called one of his friends to tell them about our argument. When he found out that I had called his friend, he was so angry that he stopped speaking to me altogether. Right after that he told me he was moving out of town, and he did. He also told me that he would give me his contact information as soon as he settled down.

That has been over six weeks ago, and I have not heard a word from him yet. I have apologized to him nonstop before he left, but it seemed to have landed on deaf ears. He has not forgiven me for that phone call to his friend. I don't want to lose him because I love him so much. I have been crying ever since he stopped speaking to me. I can't seem to pull myself together. I can't bear the fact that I might have lost him forever. I am so worried, and I am so sorry for what I did. Do you think he'll ever call me again?

Response:

Sometimes "sorry" can't fix what has been broken. It's possible that you crossed the line here. Maybe he feels you betrayed him by calling his friend after the argument. He might be disappointed in what you did and probably has loss trust in you. It really depends on what was said to the friend when you called him. If you called his friend to get advice, then that's not too bad, but if you revealed some intimate details about your relationship to his friend, then that's quite another story.

I know you are very sorry about what you did, but you can't take it back. Possibly by your actions he saw something in you that lets him know he should back up and reevaluate his relationship with you. Really, there are a number of things that could be going on with him. There is no way to know at this point if he will call you again or not. Either way, we must remember that relationships are delicate, and there are some things one must never do. Outside of abuse – whether it, be physical, mental, or emotional – one should never drag others into relationship misunderstandings. It can feel like a betrayal to your partner. You must remember the argument was between the two of you, and that's where it should stay.

Many men don't like to be pushed or pulled into a relationship with a woman. They like to make that their choice. So if he has decided it won't be you in his life, then all the pushing and calling friends and manipulating will not make it happen. If that is his choice never to call you again, then that's all it is, his choice; it is not the end of the world. Even though it may hurt you deeply, you will have to get on with your life. You said you were sorry and that's the best you can do. Learn to forgive yourself and understand that with every action there is a reaction. Whether he forgives you or not is not on you; it's on him. What you need to do is let go and move on and live your life. It may seem hard to do today, but it will get easier with each day that passes if you stay busy with your own life. You can do it.

Situation

3 I'm Not Just a Friend; We Just Had Sex

Can you believe that after we had sex he calls me and talks about another woman? He started off talking as he usually does, sweet and nice. He said "Hey, beautiful. How are you doing today?" We started talking about various things. Then he says something about a woman he met. He started saying things like, this woman was coming on to me, and she was real cute, and she was this and that.

When he first said it I thought he was just trying to see if I would get jealous. Then I thought maybe he was trying to make me jealous, or something. So I was deliberately not showing any irritation to what he was saying. Then we would talk about something else, but he would return right back to talking about this same girl again.

We ended the conversation and that was that. When he called me again, he started right back again with these other women. I told him I wasn't feeling well, and this was not the conversation I wanted to hear. He said he thought we were friends, and that's what he talks to his friends about. I said, "Yeah we were friends but we had sex remember?" I told him goodbye, and we will talk later. It's this kind of insensitivity that turns me completely off. I do think he should show me a little more respect than this.

Response:

Once a woman has sex with a man, their relationship takes on another dimension, no matter what the relationship was before. If the two of you were just friends before, then it is no longer just friend, to friend; it has another element to it. Many men are not sensitive to this change. If the two of you decide not to take it any further, he should still respect you as a woman who has had sex with him and not talk about other women in this manner to you.

If the two of you talked about other women before you had sex and it didn't seem to bother you, then you should let him know at this point in the relationship with him that you are no longer comfortable talking to him about other women. If he started talking to you about other women only after the two of you had sex, then it could be that he's trying to make you jealous. He could even be trying to put emotional distance between the two of you. In any case, men should be sensitive to any woman they have had sex with. It's just a matter of respect. But there are a lot of men who simply lose respect once they have sex with a woman. This situation is about who that man is and not about you. Maybe this is one relationship that should have stayed just friends.

Situation

4 I Will Do Any Thing to Keep This Man

I will do anything to keep him, but he doesn't know it. We have huge arguments; I say things to push him away, and he says things that really hurt me too. Usually after an argument we don't call each other for a few days. We will be fine for a while, and then it starts all over again.

See, it usually starts because he will say something to upset me, and then my temper will flare up. He tells me he loves me, and I do love him also, but we go through so much sometimes that I feel like this is all I have energy in my life to do. If I'm not fighting with him, I'm worried about the next fight we will get into.

I know this is not a very productive way to live or have a relationship. But the weird part about the whole thing is that when we are not together, I miss him so much and can't wait to see him again. It's like I fall more in love with him ever day in spite of our arguments. And I don't think he's aware of this, but I will do anything to keep this man. Yes, I know that sounds crazy, but that is how much I love him. He must love me that much too because he keeps coming back to me. I mean no matter how bad our arguments get, he comes back.

Response:

It does seem like love is weaved into some dysfunction here. I say dysfunction because of the scale you are using to measure your love. When people are use to being treated a certain way, and that way is not positive, they may very well become desensitized to their feelings. For example, if someone hurts their feelings, they know their feelings have been hurt, but they don't feel the hurt as much. That is because what these people do is rationalize or make excuses for the hurt by saying that the person who hurt them didn't mean to, and they know that the person loves them anyway. Maybe the person does love them but does not know how to express it in the right way.

When people do rationalize their feelings, they are not living the same reality that most of us are. Therefore, dysfunction can easily take place. I am saying this to you because I feel you know something is wrong with your relationship, but instead of looking at it the way it is, you are creating your own world around it. You no longer see your boyfriend abusing your feelings for him or you abusing his feelings for you. What you are seeing is, this is how we love each other.

By saying you will do any thing to keep this man, you are also saying you will do any thing to keep this abuse going on between the two of you. What the two of you need is help from someone who can put the two of you and your relationship on the right track. If you don't get counseling of some sort, your relationship is a train wreck waiting to happen. A little counseling will show the two of you how to express in a constructive way the passion that is obviously there. If the two of you are that much in love with each other, then it is worth trying to save your relationship. The two of you can make it together but you just have to learn how.

Situation

5 He Throws Women in My Face

I truly feel that if a woman didn't get a man five years ago, she's in trouble now. Men today are very cocky and will throw women in your face and think nothing about it. At least years ago they tried to hide their ways, but not now.

They brag about how women hit on them all day and how these women want them. In the very next breath they are declaring their love for you. This is bulls#*t, but this is how these men are these days; they are now in the place women used to be.

They expect the woman to treat them like the men used to treat us. This is truly what is called trading places; it's just all reversed now. It's not just in one city but all over, in every city, and every state across this whole United States. It's really disgusting that you can't find a good man anywhere anymore.

Response:

You might be right about men these days, but it's not all their fault. If women would refuse to accept this behavior from these men, then men would treat them better. But it's true; the men today will say, "If you don't accept it, the next female will," and they are right: the next female does. It's like an epidemic in this country, and women have become so desperate for a man. The woman is abandoning herself and her self-respect just to say she's got somebody. Women have become desperate, so they are spoiling the men, and therefore the men have grown to disrespect them. It is a vicious cycle: the men and the women both are out there today looking for the same thing, and it's not necessarily love that they are looking for. These days they're looking more for the money, who's got it, and how they can get some.

There's also a lot of temptation out there for men and women. If one is not grounded, these temptations can sweep one away, destroying people's lives. So it is true that things are really crazy out there now. If men and women both were stronger when faced with temptation, it would not be half as bad.

I believe the respect level has dropped for both men and women. If we can restore the level of respect for one another, especially while we are in a relationship at the time of a temptation, a lot that has been lost can eventually be restored. Most of all, true love will be restored between a good man and a good woman. If each one of us would do our tiny part in restoring real love, we will see a change in our future I am sure. Don't give up girl: I'm sure you will find your man in the not-so-distant future.

Situation

6 His Baby's Mama Drama

My boyfriend broke up with his baby's Mama a year ago. They have a three-year-old son together. He and I have been together for six months. My boyfriend and his ex spend equal time with their son. She is always dropping their son off at his apartment at all hours of the night and day.

When I am at my place and my boyfriend is at his, I never know if his ex is with him or not. This bothers me, but I don't want to seem jealous. I have been thinking that there is something else going on between them, more than his just watching their son. I got suspicious when my boyfriend started to cut his phone off at night. He says the ringing wakes his son up, and he can't get him back to sleep.

I have popped up at his apartment, but he doesn't answer the door at night either for the same reason, he doesn't want to disturb his son's sleep. He also tells me, that because his apartment is so small we would disturb his son and we would be uncomfortable trying to talk or whatever. I can't tell if he has company or not because he has a closed-in-garage, and you can't see the cars. I am concerned that his ex is spending some nights there at his place. I did ask him about this, and he told me I was crazy. He said he doesn't have time for that foolishness. His excuses are iron clad, and I can't crack them, to really find out the truth.

Response:

The only way to find out if there is more going on with

his ex or someone else is to be around him more in the evenings. This should not be a problem if he is not spending his evenings with someone else. If this is a problem for him, and he can't see you at night or you can't reach him at night, then maybe you should take a very close look at this relationship.

You should express how this alienation makes you feel when you can't reach him. If everything is on the up and up, then he should change this behavior or compromise to make you feel comfortable about all of this stuff at night. I wouldn't be too concerned about looking jealous. It's really not about jealousy; it's more about trust and your time being invested in the right place. If you are not comfortable with the way things are, then you and he will have to change them. Being involved with another person in a relationship should be about the comfort and happiness of both people. Remember, you can be miserable alone, but you want to be happy together.

Situation

7 My Weed-Head Husband

My husband and my neighbor smoke weed together. I don't smoke, so the two of them ganged up on me and told me what a square I am for not getting high with them. I am not comfortable with their relationship at all. I am 24 years old, my husband is 32 years old, and our neighbor is an attractive older woman of 47. She also has a daughter 25 years old who also gets high with them on occasion. The older woman came to me one day and said, "Tell me: why is a good man like your husband wasted on someone like you." Then she burst out in this laughter, and then said, "See you can't even take a joke."

Well, I want to see if she's still laughing after I put my foot in her old ass. My husband jumped right in and grabbed me and hugged me like it was a joke or something. I do believe my husband is having sex with her, and I believe he has had sex with her daughter too. They think I'm a young, naive fool and the joke is on me. Something's got to give; I can't take this anymore. I love my husband, but I feel they are smothering me.

Response:

I feel there may be deception on your husband's part and especially with one or both women. Your husband is not very kind or sensitive to you. He should not allow his friends to treat you this way. He is showing you no respect. This marriage needs serious counseling in order for it to work; if this doesn't take place, seriously consider your sanity in the long run.

Whether you love him or not, this relationship cannot work if the two of you are not of the same accord. You both have to want this marriage to last, or it will not work out.

Situation

8 My Friday Night Fling

I have been flirting with this guy on my job for a few weeks now. We talk at break time, and he seems to be a very nice guy. I've been thinking about inviting him over for dinner, so finally I did. I invited him over for Thursday candlelight night. That means everything is done by candlelight. He accepted my offer and was there 8:00 sharp.

We had a great dinner while scented candles were melting everywhere. One thing led to another, and we had sex. OK, so this was the first time we were alone together but everything felt so right and we really had a wonderful time. Only he wanted to have sex without the condom and I said absolutely not, but things got going and he never put the condom on. Now I'm thinking I went to bed with him so quickly and thoughtlessly, but it happened like this only because I was trying to forget my boyfriend who just broke up with me two weeks ago.

Now I'm worried that I might be pregnant. I feel a bit silly about all of this now, but what's done is done.

Response:

One night of romance and fantasy brings so many nights of worry and panic. So was it worth it?

If you are not on birth control never take a chance unless you know your cycle and when it is safe to take a chance. Plus, you really don't know this man very well, and you still did not practice safety, or insist that he does. Not only should you be worried about getting pregnant, you should be worried about getting AIDS. It would be so easy for me to advise you not to be so irresponsible with your life, but I am not you, and sometimes it is easier said than done. But putting aside all the excuses, this is serious and you can make a very big mistake doing things this way. Think about yourself and your life first.

Situation

9 The Night My Celibacy Ended

I have been celibate for eight months, so one night I went out and met a guy at a club. Well, he's in the band at this jazz club; I always go to this club almost every weekend. He plays the drums, and he is gorgeous and so sexy. I always said when I start having sex again I sure want it to be with him.

So at the end of the night, I approached this guy, and, yes, he was all of that, and, yes, and we had sex this same night. I have been practicing celibacy for the past eight months. It's not like this is something I do all the time; in fact this is the first time I had sex in eight months. So it felt like I was a virgin all over again. Everything was just wonderful; he was wonderful. Oh, yes, he was a dream.

The next morning he treated me as if we had nothing together. See, this is what gets me; it makes me so mad when men stereotype women, like the woman is a skank or slut or something if she goes to bed with him the same night. He doesn't know why the woman may have wanted to have sex with him, in the first place. These men just don't give a woman a chance to show that she really may not be like that at all. She may really be a nice girl.

Response:

Well if you wanted him for sex, then you got what you wanted, and no more thoughts about it. But if you want understanding and respect, this was not the way to get it. A man has to get to know you and then to understand you and your situation in order for him to show compassion and respect for you. And even then there is no guarantee he will respect you or even call you the next day. It really depends on the man and what he was taught about respecting women.

Don't blame him if you didn't give him a chance to know you. Remember, every action gets a reaction, so if you want to change the reaction, you must first change the action. My advice to you would have been not go to bed with him so soon. And even though you were celibate for eight months, he had just met you this night. So if you really care for him and he rejects you after the sex, it can really hurt, as it did. But with this person there will never again be another first impression for you to make. All you can do now is to hope that the two of you can become friends, and in time he will get to know you better. Hope that he will get to know the person you really are, and that is a wonderful person, I'm sure.

Situation

10 He Has Been with My Man

My friend told me he screwed my ex-boyfriend. In fact, he was quite graphic with it; he actually said, "I f#*ked him silly." Those were his exact words to me, and I will never forget it.

My boyfriend and I have been dating for four years, and we recently broke up. My friend told me this shocking news at his mother's funeral. I don't know why he chose to tell me then, maybe because he was drunk. Now that my boyfriend and I are no longer together, I guess he felt it was OK to tell me this.

My friend said this incident happened before my boyfriend and I were together. True, they were friends, but that is all I thought they were, friends not down-low brothers. Though this happened years ago, it hurt me deeply.

I couldn't believe my ears, but he said this and I heard it. I felt instant disgust for my boyfriend, and a great deception from my friend. Why did he let me live that lie about this man when he knew the truth about him? If I was his friend, how could he smile in my face every day without even giving me some sort of hint? I would never have been with this man. Just imagine what I must have felt at that moment. Even though he told me this a month ago, I am still devastated by it. How can I let go and move on without these feelings of anger, hurt, and the pain of being deceived so greatly by my best friend and my lover whom I loved very deeply?

Response:

This truly is a big one. No, I cannot imagine what you must have felt, but I do know the pain of deception from a very close friend. Breaking up from a lover whom you truly love is always very painful. But to find out that he was a lover to your best friend and your best friend is also a man, throws you into another dimension of hurt and pain.

The only reason I can give you on my part as to why he never told you until now, and why he chose to tell you at his mother's funeral, is this; Maybe he wanted to tell you sooner, but didn't want to take the chance of it getting back to your boyfriend. Maybe he chose to tell you at his mother's funeral because he didn't want his mother to find out either. Whatever reason they both chose not to tell you is between the two of them. But one thing I know for sure, knowing something like this surely would have destroyed your relationship with both your friend and your lover, as it has done now.

There is one other way to look at the reason why they didn't tell you. That could be their love for you. I know at this point this may sound bizarre to you, but if you think about it, maybe not. You're friend may have known if he told you then, when you were deeply in love with this man, it would have hurt you so much more. He told you it happened before the two of you got together and maybe it never happened again. Now your boyfriend should never have dated you in the first place. He was either being very selfish or his love for you surpassed all that went before you. This is just another way to look at it. But I do hope you realize you were the innocent person in this scenario.

Be very happy that the relationship is over and was over when you heard this devastating news. I am wishing you all the best in the future with your best friends and lovers. Just give yourself time to go through all of the feelings it takes to get through something like this, and in time you will be over it. This too will pass; you'll see.

Situation

11 The Condom Complainer

I finally had sex with this guy who has been calling me for a month. During sex he kept complaining about having to use a condom. I kept hearing him say "the condom this" and "the condom that," and he can't feel anything when he uses one.

He was so adamant about how he doesn't use one because he was in a long relationship with one woman so he didn't use one. During sex he claimed the condom broke. So if it broke then it really wasn't covering anything during sex. So in reality he still had sex with me without a condom anyway.

How can I trust this person now, after he complained about wearing one and then realizing the condom he wore had broken? How can I be sure he didn't break it on purpose? This was our first time together, and he made me very uncomfortable with him, and I really don't trust him now.

Response:

Maybe you ought to go slow with him, and watch his behavior; you may pick up clues as to his sexual lifestyle. Maybe he's telling you the truth about having one partner, or maybe he's not. It's hard to trust him at this point. His sexual style just doesn't seem very safe, and more importantly, he doesn't seem very trustworthy. I would definitely not trust him. He is showing you that he doesn't take very good care of himself either. If this behavior about condoms is like this with you, then it must be like this with others.

Situation

12 Finding A Stripper

I used to go to the strip clubs with my boyfriend; I felt if I were with him, nothing could go-down, like him getting friendly with the strippers. A male friend of ours is getting married, and my boyfriend wanted to go to a strip club to get a stripper for the bachelor party so I went with him.

There was this one stripper, when she came off the stage my boyfriend gave her a sign to come over to our table; when she came over he gave her his cell number. I knew why he gave her the number; it was for the bachelor party, but I still got upset. It made me feel very uncomfortable. I am feeling very weird about this. I keep wondering if my boyfriend is attracted to her for himself, and the bachelor party makes it all so convenient. I am not sure how to feel or think about this.

Response:

In a way there is a double message here; it's OK to go to strip clubs, and you don't mind him looking at other women as long as you're there to monitor him. But what happens when you're not there? Well, since this is a habit that's already established in your relationship, the only security you have in a situation like this is to know your man. You would have to know if he's the type that would go to the strip club without you or not.

Only you know if you can trust him or not. Is he trustworthy? If he has not given you any reason to believe he wants a stripper, and you know your man loves you, then I don't think you have much to worry about. Remember, it's a bachelor party, and that's all it is.

Have you and your man ever discussed fantasies he may have? Maybe this way you can get a glimpse into some of the things he's thinking and dreaming about. If you knew these things, you would be able to understand a lot better why he does the things that he does.

Situation

13 My Husband Never Calls Me From the Office

My husband and I have a strange relationship in my opinion. We have been married for two years. We have a two-year-old son. My husband has never called me from the office to say "Hello" or "How are things going at home." Whenever I call him, he could never be reached. He works in a security plant, so I do understand. But what puzzles me is whenever I call him at lunch he still never answers his telephone.

When he comes home from work, he eats dinner and goes straight to his computer. He stays there until midnight and sometimes longer. This goes on every night.

Recently a friend of my husband who works with him dropped me a hint. He told me my husband was getting a new secretary again. I asked why, and he told me that this girl was just like the last one. I didn't understand what he meant, but he then said, "I think she liked him or he liked her or something like that." I asked my husband's friend to please be honest with me and tell me if something was going on or not. He looked at me and said, "Honestly, I don't know for sure, but it has been rumored that they were, but you will have to find that out on your own."

This left me puzzled because why would he tell me something like this, and just leave it. I thought maybe he was trying to start trouble between my husband and me. Then I thought, am I in denial or what? This bothered me for a while.

One day I ask my husband how was his secretary getting along at the job. He looked at me a little strange and said, " This one has to leave." I then asked why and he answered, "How should I know?" Well I thought, if he's her boss he should know. I felt that he gave me the wrong answer. As I recall this is about the third of fourth secretary in two years. They all have been very beautiful women, from what I know. Do you think these women and my husband have been having affairs and then he fires them and gets a new one? I really feel this is what's going on.

Response:

This would be a clever way of cheating wouldn't it? I don't know if that is what's been going on, but if it is, then maybe that is why they have left or been fired after only being there a few months. The only way to get some clear understanding on this issue is to go to the personnel department at your husband's job and inquire.

You can ask for the reason why your husband has had three or four secretaries in only two years. You may be able to see a pattern or similar reasons why they left the company. Some companies will not disclose this information to anyone. Every job has different policies.

The strangeness of your husband's staying on the computer every evening until midnight could be a clue. Sometimes when there's a pattern like this, there could be communication with other women through the Internet. Maybe you should start inquiring about what he's doing on the computer every night until late. One way or another, now that you're on to it, I'm sure you will fine your answer, and there will be closure to the strangeness of this relationship.

Situation

14 My Boyfriend Competes with Me

I am tired of my boyfriend competing with me. It seems like if I buy anything new, he has to get something new also. This is so childish to me, and I have told him this also. I have confronted him with this, but he turns it back on me saying I compete with him.

Besides that, we are in a loving relationship and have been together for three years. I am to the point where I hate to let him know my progress at work, or anything good that happens for me, period. This saddens me because I do love him and I want to share the good things as well as the bad things, but I just can't take this competition thing.

He shows little or no support for my successes. It is like success should only be for him, and making personal progress should not be mine.

Response:

This should let you know that if he is not happy or supportive of you now, he will not be in the future either. If the two of you are seriously thinking about a future together, then maybe a little counseling about this issue should be the answer. And if the two of you love each other but this is the only thing between the two of you, then try and get rid of this problem fast, and have a happy future together. If this is not dealt with, then this could be the time bomb, ready to explode at any time.

Jealousy and competition should not be between two people who are in a so-called loving relationship. Why fight each other when there are so many things to fight against in the world. If this does not get straight with the two of you, there won't be much progress in your relationship, ever.

Situation

15 He Wants A Threesome

This guy and I had been dating for five years. A year-and-a-half ago, we broke up. Recently he called me. I was surprised to hear from him because we broke up very upset with each other. He asked me if he could take me out for a drink sometime. I said yes, next Friday would be fine. So we went out for drinks.

We both had a good time and wanted to see each other again. So we did see each other again and again for a month. One night he called me and asked if I would do something for him that only special people do; I asked him what was it, and he said this: Will I have sex with him and his male cousin?

I was shocked that he would ask me something like this. My second thought was that I know he is joking. But he wasn't; he really wanted me to do this. I knew we were really over now. I thought to myself, his male cousin, or did he mean a male friend? This sounds like some gay S#$t, and if it is a cousin then it is some gay incest S#$t, Yuck!

Whatever this is, it is definitely not for me. Now all of this is just too much for me to even think about. So is this why he came back around, to invite me into this nasty world of his? I wish he would stay gone this time forever.

Response:

Wow! Now that does seem like a lot to hear from your friend after a month of dating. This is probably part of his lifestyle now. It could have been part of his life style before also. One never knows these days for sure. If the two of you were going to be together again, he needed to let you know what he was into now.

I guess this was his way of telling you he was bisexual. Now that you know, you have made your decision to leave him alone. It is better that you know the truth. He could have kept this part of himself a secret, and you could have found out in a more devastating way.

I'm sure you didn't want to bust in on him and his male cousin, did you? Now that would be a blow to your head, your mind, and your heart. Just say Good-Bye to Mr./ Ms. - whatever -Nasty. If this is not your thing, just be glad he's gone and stays gone.

Situation

16 He Beat My Ass Last Night

I'm stuck in the house because of my black eye, swollen lip, and bruises all over. I am embarrassed to go out. He came over to my house last night and beat my ass. It's been over between us for three months now.

His wife finally called me. She must have found my number on his cell phone. She wanted to know if I'm the same person she caught him with a while ago. I was so angry with him for lying to me about their relationship in the first place. I told her, "Yes, I am the one."

He told me that they were separated, and would soon be divorced. This was a big-ass lie, and at the time I had no reason not to believe him. I was so angry with him for lying to me that I told her everything.

First she didn't believe me, but after I told her every date and time she was out of town in the last year, she started to believe me then. When I described her home and especially her bedroom to her, the B#*+h was frozen with shock. I guess she confronted his ass about this issue. He probably thought he got away clean. I guess he felt he would teach me a lesson by coming over to my house and beating me the way that he did.

Response:

So what are you going to do? Have you considered your safety? The questions can go on forever in a situation like this. My main concern at this point is for your safety. Go some place where you feel safe and are around people you can trust. Stay there until you can deal with what you're going to do about this situation.

When you found out that he was married, you should have ended this relationship. It was a relationship built on deception, so how could it turn out right? You should not have gone along with this once you did find out he was married. There is so much that is wrong in this whole thing. Pointing fingers won't undo any of this mess now.

This man is her husband, so you can see why she is upset. I don't think it was right for you to try and hurt her the way you did by describing her home and her bedroom to her. Remember, the two of you did wrong to her. The person who should be blamed is that knucklehead man who lied in the first place. You know this is something that men have done throughout the ages, saying they're single, when they're very married, so it's not new. But it is up to the women who they approach to be clever enough to spot when something is just not right. It is sad that the woman has to be the one to be defensive and skeptical when a man approaches her. But it has come down to just that. They're just so many games out there. Not only do men play them, but women play them also. In order not to get caught up in them, one must be wise.

Situation

17 He Found Out the Baby Is His

My man and I have been dating for two years now. He has a nine-year-old son by his ex-wife, and he just found out that his ex-girlfriend's baby girl is really his child. The baby is a year and a few months old.

My man did come to me and explain this to me. He told me he had no idea this baby was his. When we met, he had recently broken up with her. When he left her, he had no idea she was pregnant. I do believe him, but where does that leave us now?

I have no children, but I do want children in the future, but now I don't know if he will want anymore, children. Besides that, I now will have to deal with two baby-mama-dramas if we stay together. This may truly be too much for me. He's beginning to show a lot of attention to his ex and their baby; I guess he has to, but I feel like I've lost everything, and she's gained everything. I really feel lost right now.

Response:

I can truly understand why you feel the way you do. It's sort of a shock to you it seems. It does mean altering your relationship a bit. It's obvious this man wants to be a part of this child's life, and whether or not there is drama between you and the mothers of his children, remember you are still his woman. How you handle the situation would be up to your man and you to decide.

He will have to set the pace of respect and order for you three women, since he is the one dealing with all three of you. Once everyone knows his and her boundaries, then I believe you and your man can still have a great life together. It is still you and your man's relationship that should be your main concern. Just don't give your power in the relationship over to anyone else. Remember, even though you don't have children in this relationship, it doesn't make you any less important in his heart.

Situation

18 He Stopped Calling Right After Sex

I agreed to have sex with this guy I met a while ago. We went out on a few dates together and had a great time. So we decided to have sex. I told him to wear a condom, and he looked shocked. I said, "Why are you looking like that?" He said, "We know each other; it's not like a one-night stand or anything."

He kept asking me to tell him why I wanted him to wear a condom. I still insisted he wear one. He then asked me if there was something that I needed to tell him. I said "No." He did put it on, but he never called me after that.

I called him and I asked him if there was something wrong, He said, " I am not sure about things, and I'm not sure about you." I believe he is afraid that I may have a disease or something. I'm just really puzzled about his behavior toward me.

Response:

It might be that he believes you have something or it might be another reason why he hasn't called. But the reason he gave you was that he wasn't sure about you. This seems a little backwards since he's the one who was going to have sex without the condom. Well, the way things were left could keep you puzzled and never really knowing the cause of his behavior, but know that you did the right thing by insisting he wear a condom.

Even if you knew him a while before having sex with him, you did the right thing. As long as you don't have a disease and you just want to be safe, then you are taking care of you. That is a responsibility you have to yourself, to take care of yourself. Whether you see him again is your own choice. Maybe you should consider his behavior a warning sign. He could be one of those guys who is careless about his sex life. If this is the case, this can be a problem in the long run. Whatever you decide to do, be strong, and continue to be safe.

Situation

19 The Lover I Met on Vacation

I have been talking to a man I met on my vacation last year. He lives in another state, but we've talked on the phone about twice a week for the last year.

This has given us a chance to get to know each other somewhat. He told me he was coming to my city and he wanted to see me. Well he came and I saw him and we had great sex. That was a month ago, and today he called me for the first time since that day. It has been one month, and this is the first call I got from him. I didn't answer his call; I let it go to my voicemail. This is what he said: " Well, hello sweetie; give me a call back when you get this message," I am feeling hurt, used, and insulted. If I call him back, how do I react? Angry? Or do I act as if his behavior didn't affect me? Or do I call back at all?

Response:

With this type of behavior, he is showing you he is not very serious about you and him. Now, if this is what you are looking for, someone who will see you when he is in town and not even phone you until a month later, then you can respond to his call. But if there is more on your mind for this relationship, then I would say this is not it and don't waste your time. But this is a choice you will have to make. Maybe you should call him back to put closure to this. But that would be the only reason I would call him back.

Situation

20 If He's Deceiving Me, He's Damn Good

My boyfriend goes out with his boys all the time. They just hang out, and I don't try to stop that. He knows that I am at home waiting for him to get back, or to call, or whatever. I have become very suspicious of him at times.

I don't want to accuse him of doing anything wrong because I really don't see him doing anything. If he is deceiving me, he is damned good at it. I'm beginning to feel he has me just where he wants me.

I'm always at home waiting for him. I enjoy making my boyfriend feel comfortable about our relationship, but I can't seem to find the balance. I need to find a balance of making him feel secure and him not taking me for granted.

Response:

I hope you still have maintained relationships with your girlfriends while dating this guy. It is very important to have your friends while you're in a relationship. If your boyfriend goes out with his friends and leaves you home, then maybe you should go out to a movie or dinner with your girlfriends, your mom, or your sisters.

This will let him know you have other interests also. This will also let him know that you are not going to sit around waiting for him to get back or call or whatever. I do believe if your boyfriend is deceiving you, it will come out sooner or later. If you keep yourself busy, he may become less busy with his boys. He may want more together time with just you and him. Being isolated in any relationship is never a good idea, so just stay connected to people who also want the best for you. They are those who love you too, like family and close friends.

Situation

21 The X-Ray Sex Vision Thing

hat I will never understand is why would a man want to f#*k without a condom, especially if he just wants to hit it and he thinks the woman is a scank? Tell me why? Do you know the answer? Why would you risk dying for 20 minutes of sex?

That's just down right dumb. These dumb-ass men act like they have this x-ray sex vision thing going, where they can tell just by looking at a woman if she has a disease or not. They say if she looks like she has something, they just don't deal at all.

This is a very dumb answer once again, like they can pick out the person who has a disease or not. So there they go fighting not to wear a condom, not only is this dumb it's nasty.

Then you may hear them say she looks like a good girl, so it's OK not to wear a condom. But what these boys better remember is that good girls get bad diseases from nasty men, men who didn't wear a condom, and good guys get bad diseases from nasty girls who are with these men who don't wear condoms. Not only are there dumb-ass men, but there are dumb-ass women too, women who don't want the man to wear the condom because they claim they can't feel him with one on.

But don't they get it? Don't they know that a disease doesn't know what a person looks like and doesn't care what a person looks like? It will attack you just the same. Come on, now; what someone looks like has nothing to do with wearing a condom or not wearing one. Wear one because even pretty people die, don't they? So tell me, please, why don't these dumb-ass folks ever "get it"? I guess they will finally "get it," when the doctor informs them that now they better "get" a way to live with AIDS or some other incurable thing.

Response:

I can see your point, and you are absolutely right, and with so much going on these days, you would think they would know better. You can never be too careful with your life; you only get one. Even if you are in a monogamous relationship, you can't be a hundred percent sure you're safe without a condom either. The only thing one can be sure of is that you are at risk if you don't protect yourself by wearing a condom. It's sure better to be safe than sorry. One may think, If only we could trust our partners, but sadly, that's rare these days.

Situation

22 Our Twisted Honeymoon Bed

My fiancé asked me something that blew my mind. My fiancé is a physically beautiful man in every way. I love him deeply, and he loves me, but he has one wish for our honeymoon night and that is for us to take another person to our honeymoon bed with us.

He wants us to take another woman to our honeymoon bed. At first I thought he was crazy, or does he think I am? He knows I will do absolutely anything for him, but this? After some time of thinking about it, and his explaining how important this is to him, I have been considering it.

He has told me this will be the one and only time this will ever happen. He also told me on that night he will tell me something he has never told me before but only after I have made love to this woman. That's right; he wants me to make love to a woman, something I have never done before. He has promised me he will not touch her; he just wants her and me to have sex, but he will be there. He told me this would be the completion of consummating our marriage vows.

It will only be for this one night and the woman will be my choice. We will visit many strip clubs to find her, we will pay her, and she will never see us again. This may sound crazy, but I am considering it.

Response:

If this is something that may be against your morals, then regardless of what he wants, this is something you should not do. If this is something you want to do, then this is your choice as an adult.

This doesn't seem like something that is cut and dry; this seems like there's more to it than just this one night. If I were you, I would definitely ask some questions about his making a request like this.

The first thing I would be concerned about is why he is suggesting such a thing of me; the next thing that would concern me would be if he is straight, bisexual, homosexual, or just a freak. Maybe you need to know him better than you do before entering a marriage. You need to know what you are dealing with, and I don't think you do. I hope the two of you have really considered what marriage is all about, especially if you're planning on having children.

Your relationship may need some serious looking at. This foundation sounds shaky at this point. Maybe he wants you to do this thing he has requested because he has some things in his past that are similar to this. Maybe that something he has to tell you after you engage in this behavior is that he has been with other men. I say this only because this is such an odd request for a honeymoon night. This is something you must seriously think about, and please think hard.

Situation

23 His Cell Phone Called My Phone Number

is cell phone called my cell phone. I answered and said hello; no one answered back but I could hear him talking to a woman, and they were in the car driving. I then listened to what I was hearing and from the conversation it seems as if they were going to the movies.

The woman kept saying, "OK, baby, what would you like to see?" Then he said to her, "I don't really care; I'll leave that up to you." Then he said to her, "you're so beautiful you could have any man you want and I know you have a lot of money so why even trip on those people?" Then I heard her say, "Yeah, but they are going to give me my damn money, and I'm not playing with them." They went into the movies, and the phone cut off.

He and I had just broken up about two weeks before this. I'm not sure if this was a set up call, or if it was for real. It's hard to tell with him because he does stuff like that; if we got upset or argued with each other, he would go out with a woman to upset me.

Usually he says nothing ever happens, but that is one of the reasons why our relationship did not work. He had no remorse about doing this kind of a thing to me; he would run to some woman every time we got into a conflict or some kind of misunderstanding.

This time I'm not going to go running back as usual. I am tired of going through this. In the last two weeks, I have not answered any of his calls. I do love him very much, and, yes, this hurts very much, but I am through with all of his trauma-causing-drama reeking havoc on my life. S#%t. This time I am done. For-Real-Done.

Response:

By your telling me your situation, I can really see why you would be done. That's a very good thing that you have made up your mind to stand up for yourself and not allow this to continue in your life. This kind of a man is what I call damaged goods. See, he has lost his sensitivity to women. If a man threatens you with behavior like this whenever the two of you get into an argument or a misunderstanding and especially without remorse, there is not much there for you to work with. A man like this needs so much work to get his head screwed on straight that it would be up to you to decide if you want to invest that much time and energy into it, and still there is no guarantee.

About your wondering if the call to your phone was real or not, let me know; even though you say you're done, you may not be sure you are. If he's done this to you before and on more than one occasion, then this is his pattern, and he doesn't seem to be changing it for you or the relationship. He sounds like he has deep controlling issues, and it probably would be an exhausting life trying to be in a relationship with this type of a man, not to mention a very hurtful life and absolutely one without trust.

Well, if you want to go through this and continuously, then, go back to him. But if you want respect and peace of mind, then maybe it's best to stay done with him.

Situation

24 He Will Call Me Right Back, and That Was Yesterday

We had great sex a few nights ago, but he has not called me since he left my house that night. On the third night I couldn't take it anymore, so I called him. He answered the phone and in a pleasant voice said, "Hey, babe; let me call you right back; I'm busy." I said O.K., but he has not called back and that was yesterday.

He has been acting distant with me for a few weeks now. I asked him what was wrong, and he said nothing is wrong. He added it has nothing to do with me, but there is a big difference in his behavior toward me. The only thing that I feel it could be is when we had that big argument a month ago I said a few things I really didn't mean.

I asked him for his forgiveness, and he said he did forgive me. But the way he has been treating me shows me something has really changed forever. I do feel it's my fault for this change. I wish I could take back the whole argument. I am sorry about this and the way things are turning out.

Response:

The good thing is that you recognize what you did wrong and you do feel remorse. Maybe you're right that there were some things said in the argument that affected his feelings toward you, and as a result has put shade on the relationship. If he chooses not to tell you exactly what the problem is, then you'll probably never really know.

Maybe this relationship wasn't going to go far anyway, especially if it seems to be ending like this and without a clearer understanding of things. That is why I always say watch your words because once a word is spoken, especially when we are angry, it can never be taken back. It is good to keep in mind that when you argue, make sure whatever you say you really mean, or just don't say it.

Relationships and friendships can be ruined forever if the wrong words are spoken or meanings are misunderstood. People are in our lives for a reason; it could be a good reason or not but they are there. I have found that they are there because they usually have something to teach us about life and especially about our own life. Whether we recognize it or not, when they leave there will be a lesson there. If we don't get the lesson, we will repeat it; if not through the same person, it will be through someone else. But, believe me, life will make sure you learn it one way or another. Maybe through your words you are learning a lesson from life. Maybe the lesson this time is to watch your words because you can injure a good relationship by being careless with what you have said to someone you care deeply about. I know it hurts, but hopefully the two of you can work it out.

Situation

25 Is That Really His Cousin?

This woman came over to my boyfriend's apartment at 11:00 p.m. a few nights ago. She knocked on the door, and he jumped out of bed to see who it was. It was the same woman who has come by many times before. She has been coming by his apartment off and on from the beginning of our relationship, and we've been together for seven months now.

Anyway, he came back into the room and grabbed his jacket then said to me, "Oh, it's my cousin again; she needs to talk to me. He left the room so fast that I didn't get a chance to respond. He went outside for a few minutes and came back in to tell me he would be a while longer. After ten minutes or so I looked out to see what was going on. They were sitting in her car, so I couldn't really see from the bedroom window what was really going on.

When he came back in, he said nothing. I then asked him, "What's going on; is she ok?" again, no response. Since then I have found birthday cards and a few love notes from her to him. If she is really a cousin, there seems to be something fishy going on.

He insists that this woman is his cousin, and how dare I think it's anything else. I really don't know what to think. But I know this does not feel right to me. It seems like she will always be around us if we stay together. This is so weird to me. Doesn't it sound weird to you too?

Response:

Maybe this is the perfect example of kissing cousins; no, I'm just kidding. You are right; this does sound pretty weird. Well, maybe you will never really know the truth. You may only be able to speculate because if there is deception here, they could be very clever in disguising whatever it is. It is possible that she is an ex-lover or it's some homey girlfriend thing.

If you have a disturbing gut feeling, you may have to wait and find out if she is his cousin or not. If she is his cousin, then they do have a strange and even weird way of relating to each other. I don't know any cousins who relate to each other like this unless there is some funny stuff going on between them, and you know what I am talking about.

How is his relationship with other members of his family? Someone else in the family should be able to tell you if she is a cousin or not. If it turns out that she is his cousin, then their relationship really needs some serious boundaries. If it turns out that she was an old girlfriend, then I would say they call themselves playing you. Whatever this turns out to be, you will be uncomfortable until you finally know the truth. Girl, whatever it is, when you find out you will have to get back to me and let me know because it would be too much to know he is having an affair with his own cousin. Yuck!

Situation

26 Take It With A Grain Of Salt

He and I work together; therefore, I cannot avoid seeing him in the office. We had sex for the first time last weekend. He speaks to me when we are at work, but he has not called me at all this week.

We both act as if nothing happened. It's because he didn't call me all week that I concluded he was not really interested in me. The other day I was talking to another male co-worker, and all of a sudden, you-know-who acted interested. He was showing me attention, and especially when other people were around, he was pouring it on. I don't quite know how to take this.

Response:

Take this with a grain of salt. He is just doing the territorial thing now. Some men do this to let other men know they are interested so that the other men can back off. This man feels he has rights over the other man at this point. I believe it's just a man thing.

If he were truly interested in you for the right reasons, he would have called sooner, especially since the two of you see each other every day at work. It's better to see the truth about his feelings for you now than to drag it out into something it's not. Don't you agree?

Situation

27 He's Obsessing Over His Ex

My man and his ex broke up three years ago. He and I have been dating for two years now. He has always had a hard time with the fact that his daughter lives out of state with her mother. They moved away a year ago. There are times when he needs to talk about how he misses his little girl.

The conversation will move from the daughter to the daughter's mother sometimes. It always starts out with him saying my daughter's mother is a B#*#h. This is because she won't let him speak to his daughter. There are times when he goes into such detail about this or that, an hour may go by and we haven't said anything about us.

He insists that I give him feedback about her because I am a woman. He asks me what I think she's thinking, or what do I think she's doing. I am so tired of this; I think he is still very much in love with her. Now that she's told him she is getting married, he has gone crazy about it. He is definitely driving me crazy. He complains that he doesn't want his daughter to be raised by another man and so on. I don't know what else to say to him, and I just can't get him to stop obsessing over his ex and the things she does.

If she wants to get married and start another family, can you please tell me why should he be so upset? I know it's not about another man raising his daughter because this same man has been in his daughter's life for more than a year now. Could it be what I think it is, that he is obsessing over his ex because he still cares and if she gets married he knows that's pretty final?

Response:

Well, you might be right about him obsessing over something concerning this matter. But he may truly be concerned about his daughter as well. It may feel a little like he is losing his daughter to another man because the other man will be his daughter's stepfather, and he will be in her life on an everyday basis. Or maybe the fact that she's getting married is making him jealous. There could be many unresolved feelings here for him. It all depends on how they broke up and the reason why.

But your man has to realize his ex has moved on in her life. He also must realize that he will always be in his daughter's life because he is her father. And if he is there for her when she needs him, no other man will be able to take his place. If her getting married is something he just found out about, then give him a little time to adjust. It was his ex and his child is involved.

You should let him know that, besides his daughter, the only relationship he should be concerned with is the one with you and him. The other woman is gone, and I don't think she is coming back. If there are no other complaints about the relationship but this one, I'm sure a little more time will resolve it.

Your boyfriend will just have to grow up and realize that the relationship with his ex is over, and he should focus on the one at hand. He should realize you are there and you are ready to start a new life with him. But if he doesn't realize it soon, he may have two ex women. I hope the two of you can work this out.

Situation

28 She Liked Him, but He Liked Me

I was visiting a friend of mine and she told me she was inviting some friends over. Then she said there was this one guy that she was inviting, and she really liked him. She said she was hoping that one day they would be together. Then I said, "So the two of you are into each other?" She said, "No, he hasn't shown me that he cares like that."

When her friends came over I met the guy she was talking about. We all played music and cooked and ate excellent food. We had wonderful drinks, and the evening was great. Then the guy my friend likes started to hit on me. I told him that I felt uncomfortable talking to him because he and my girlfriend liked each other.

He then made it very clear that he did not care for her in that way at all. No doubt, I was attracted to this very fine man. My friend could see we both were very attracted to each other, and I could see she was not very happy about this. But I kept thinking, if they don't have any thing between them, then why let a good man get away, right? So I continued to show interest. I don't want to lose her as a friend, but I am truly attracted to this man.

Response:

This is a difficult position to be in. If she is a very good friend, then she should understand that if he doesn't want her and he is attracted to you, then why try to block it? She probably feels very disappointed or even hurt by his attraction to you. So try to understand your friend's point of view. But she should face the fact that if he is not attracted to her in that way, the two of them will probably never be more than friends.

You may have to decide that if you deal with him, you may lose her friendship, especially since she told you before you met him that she was interested in him. She probably figured the two of you would be attracted to each other, and that could be why she told you of her feelings for him in the first place.

The wisest thing for her to do is not stand in between her two friends who are attracted to each other. This way the three of you can remain friends. But if she breaks friendship with you, and you stay connected to Mr. Fine, then it's possible she loses both you and him as friends. Now, if her feelings for this man are really strong, then it may not be that easy for her to let go of the thought of the two of them being together someday. You will have to decide if a relationship with this man means more to you than your friendship with this woman. It is something to think about.

Good luck in your choice.

Situation

29 Jealousy in A Long Distance Relationship

I am in a long-distance love relationship. We have been dating for four months now, and I am so in love with him and know he's in love with me too.

We are 1,500 miles apart; we talk every day; he checks on me, and I do the same. The other day he called me, and I couldn't get to my cell phone fast enough because I had it on silent.

I was in a movie theater, so when I checked my cell, it was two hours later. He left so many messages, and they all were hurtful. We have been separated for three weeks, and these are the types of things he said in his messages to me. "So you're too busy to answer your phone, I see; this is what I am talking about. You are f*#king up; maybe I need to go back with my baby's mother."

The rest of the messages were like this too, and this messed with me because his baby's mother lives right there in the same city that he is in now. First, I am shocked that he would go off like that. He has always been so sweet. What do you think all of this is about?

Response:

Long distant relationships are really hard to maintain these days. He could be feeling the pressure of your not been near him. He is probably feeling a bit insecure about the fidelity in the relationship. He probably feels you're lonely and will seek companionship somewhere else, but if the two of you are serious about each other and you have plans to live in the same city in the near future, then it could work.

Trust and patience are the ingredients that will hold this relationship together, but without these a long-distance relationship will crumble. You should be concerned about these accusations because it shows a clue to what's underneath all that sweetness he's been laying on you. There seems to be some insecurity, and a hot temper, splashed with a little meanness here.

These accusations on the phone may destroy your relationship before you two even get to that point of being together. Maybe you should give this relationship a little more time to see if this person is what you really want. Threats about his baby's mother are not good, and with behavior like this, maybe he's covering up for something he's already doing. A question you need to ask him, if you haven't asked already is, what is the relationship between the baby's mother and him? Don't be surprised if he's still seeing her. My advice to you is look hard before you leap 1,500 miles into a nightmare.

Situation

30 Men Are Like Animals: Show Fear They'll Attack

I don't know what I'm doing wrong; I just can't take this anymore. I have had four quick boyfriend flings in the last six months. Then they just seem to fade out. My sister told me I am a little too needy and I am running them off because I'm not letting the man do his man thing.

She said, "Sometimes men need to be with men; it doesn't mean that he's leaving you or that he doesn't want to be with you." But when he wants to spend this time with his friends, I usually panic. It makes me feel that he is turning away from me. I must admit I get insecure, so I start calling them nonstop until he picks up the phone.

If I don't get him, I will leave messages on his service telling him how I feel. My sister said that I am chasing him down. It shows my fear and my insecurity. This is what makes it bad for you she said; once a man knows how afraid you are to lose him; that fool will keep you afraid that he will leave you; he will be doing all sorts of things just to keep control over you. My sister said men are like animals; show fear and they will attack you. If a man knows you are afraid of something, he will give you more of it to keep you where he wants you.

Response:

Maybe your sister has been with men like this. But all men are not like this. Your sister could be saying that if you show how insecure you are to some men, they my use this as leverage to keep you in line. Or they want to keep some sort of control over you. There are a lot of women who are beautiful and have no reason to be insecure, but because they don't realize their beauty or they don't know who they are, they will show how insecure they are about themselves.

Sometimes when you show you have these types of insecurities within, a man may become puzzled as to why you are so insecure; especially if he sees you as beautiful and that you have so much going on. It is this that may cause him to question if you are really all that he believes you were. He might say if you are truly the woman he thought you were, then why are you so afraid of losing little old him?

This could cause him to act differently towards you because he is now looking at you with question or doubt in his mind. I can't say what the reason is that you can't hold a man, but if you are acting insecure, that could be part of it. Sometimes there is something going on inside of a man that he has to be deal with first. Try and find out what is the root of your fear, then you would probably show a more secure behavior with men. Instead of your actions making them feel uncomfortable, your more secure actions will make them feel comfortable and more secure in a relationship with you. A really good relationship starts out when two people feel really good about themselves first.

Situation

31 I Was Shocked by What I Heard

M y boyfriend is my heart, and he is very adorable. He is
also a very big flirt. Women are drawn to his flirtatious
ways. So one night my girlfriend and I thought it
would be fun to call him and I wanted her to act like some
other girl. I wanted to see what he would say, if he thought he
was talking to some other woman.

We called on three-way, and she started flirting with him.
I was listening on my phone. I knew my boyfriend had gone
to this club so my girlfriend said that he gave her his phone
number. He said, "Great, I'm glad you called." Then he said,
"Wait, are you the lawyer that I walked to her car?" My
girlfriend said, "Yes, I am her," and he jumped in and said,
"Oh, my God, I am so glad you called me; I didn't think you
would."

Well by this time I was really pissed, hearing this on the
other end of the phone, and I didn't want to say a word
because I now wanted to hear whatever else he was going to
say to the lawyer he so badly wanted to call him. My girlfriend asked him if he has a girlfriend? He said," Yes, but we
are breaking up; we don't really click. " He went on to say, "
I'm looking to move on, get married, and have kids." I was
devastated from what I heard. I knew it was over for him and
me now.

My heart was immediately broken and I did not want for
us to end, but after this how could I stay? I asked myself,
could he have said this to my girlfriend because he was tipsy
or high and was just in a flirty mood? I wanted to believe this,

but deep inside I knew better. He was out there giving other women his phone number.

It was obvious what he had been doing behind my back. It was as if I was listening to a totally different person. He didn't seem like the same man I knew. It's been over between us for a month now, and I am still shocked by what I have found out about him. It seems like I will never get over this because it hurts so much.

Response:

I'm sure anyone would be shocked and devastated by hearings such things. Whether he was high or not, he is still a flirt. You being on the other end of the phone while your girlfriend pretended to be someone else; is deceptive also. When doing something like this, you must be prepared for anything. You set him up, but you also set yourself up too. You wanted to know how he is when you are not around. Well, now you know. It's that old cliché, curiosity killed the cat, and his knowing cannot bring him back.

Now that you know how he is when you are not around, do you feel better within? By doing what you did you heard things you never thought you would hear, and therefore the relationship is truly damaged for you. On the other hand, you found out what type of a man you had and now you can let him go and you can move on. This way you won't be wasting your time with him anymore. Isn't it better to know he's a flirt than not know the truth and believe a lie? I know you are still hurt, and it may take a while before you can completely get over it, but trust that you will and you will be better off without a man like this.

Situation

32 She Said I Couldn't Handle Him

I graduated in June with my B.A. degree, and in January I landed this great job out of town. I befriended a woman who was old enough to be my mother, but she was real cool I thought. A few months later my fiancé came to town to be with me. He met my friends at work and everything was fine.

One day this woman I had befriended told me that my fiancé and I would not be together long. She said I could not handle a man like that, indicating he was too much man for me. She said, "Girl, I am your friend; I'm just telling you the truth."

One afternoon about a month later, my fiancé came to pick me up from work. That same afternoon this woman's daughter came to pick her up from work. She introduced her daughter to my fiancé. After that day they established a close friendship; whenever we are at work and my fiancé and her daughter are there also, they were always talking together. My womanly instincts are telling me they have a relationship going on right under my nose. My fiancé denies everything. There is just too much eye contact and an overall feeling that they are into each other; it shows when they are in the same room. I'm just not sure how to handle this without making myself look like I am jealous of this woman's daughter.

Response:

This does sound suspicious, especially if this woman that you befriended would make a statement like that to you. To answer your question, yes, it seems like this woman had her daughter in mind the whole time. Your fiancé is not being very honorable toward his commitment to you as your fiancé.

At this point you will have to be very observant and listen to your intuition. It might be telling you to take a closer look at your husband-to-be. There is really nothing much you can do if they are not showing you any thing directly. But usually something like this will come out if they continue being lovers or whatever they are. Just be prepared for anything with a fiancé that could be so callous about your feelings.

Situation

33 I Am in Love with A Fool

I am in love with a fool. I know he loves me as much as I love him. He got upset with a response of mine; he took it the wrong way. He said I really hurt him.

It's been two months, and he won't come back to me. I am broken hearted because he just won't give me a chance to explain. He said there is no need for explaining. What could he be thinking to be so absolutely stubborn about this? He just is not giving us a chance to talk this thing out. How do I let go? How do I move on? Or how do I get him back into my life? He is acting foolish to me.

Response:

Maybe there is more to it than you know. Maybe he is using that as an excuse to break up with you anyway. Maybe he never intended to make you and him a reality. So he chose to put the blame on you and cowardly walk away. The fact that he loves you should make him want to talk to you about this. I don't really know what it was that he really didn't understand or what caused him to turn away, but I can only say this. If someone turns away from you because of a misunderstanding and he doesn't try to correct or understand the problem, then there must be a lot of immaturity within that person. If this is how he solves problems, then there probably would be many misunderstandings in your relationship with him.

There is obviously a problem somewhere. There is an inability to solve problems or confront problems or something. So maybe you should thank your lucky stars that he made his exit. Now you should focus on actually letting this go and looking for a more emotionally mature man: a man who will tell you what's wrong with him and handle his business like a grown up.

Situation

34 The Wanna-Be Architect

He is a pretty-boy type, always sharp from head to toe; I am proud to bring him around my friends because he really makes me look good. When he approached me, we were at a stoplight. He hollered, "Could I have your number?" I hollered back, yeah, so we pulled over and he got out of his car and I really liked what I saw. I didn't get out of my car; he came to my car window. We exchanged numbers, and I couldn't wait until he called. To be honest with you if he didn't call me within that week, I would have called him.

When we talked, he told me he was a graduate of a university out of state. He said he was an architect. We went out a few times before he told me he lost his job. Then as time went on, he told me he didn't exactly go to a university for his degree. It was a trade school instead. He started to ask me if I would loan him a few bucks here and there. I did for a while, and then I noticed he was getting high. When I confronted him, he said he was doing it because he was depressed. To me this whole thing was just getting worse.

We got into an argument one day, and he asked why I wouldn't help him out financially because I could afford to. Then he said that's why he spoke to me in the first place, because I was driving the right car. Then he added he wouldn't talk to a woman like me because I'm a little too heavy for his liking. I have been on a diet and lost 35 lbs., and at the time of this argument I was weighing 165 lbs. I don't know how to handle this because I thought we both loved each other; I know I really love him. I am not ready to just let him go.

Response:

Well, after statements like those, you should realize his motives are not right. He expects you to give him money, and it seems like this is not about love. He is looking for some sort of a handout. The architect thing turned out to be a big lie. There is a lot of deception from him. He sounds like one big con artist to me. I would say see it for what it is, and I'm sure you could do better than this want-to-be-an-architect perpetrator.

Look, there are a lot of men who go after women who they think can take care of them. They may need a car or a place to stay or their cell bill paid. You know they have to keep the cell on so they can talk to the women they really want during the day while you are at work making the money to take care of him. Don't be his fool. No matter how fine he is, remember this is his job – he's working to keep you paying.

Situation

35 The Rough-Neck in my Apartment Complex

I have been dating a very sexy, beautiful, roughneck who lives in my apartment complex. We have been kicking it for a few months now. It has been great, and we have great times together, plus the sex is off the hook. He came to me a couple of weeks ago, and told me a friend of his was coming to visit him and she needed a place to stay, and he told her she could stay with him. He said it would only be for a few days. I have seen pictures of this girl and she is beautiful.

I am really not sure if their relationship is just friends or if there was more at one time. I told him I did not feel comfortable with her staying with him, and he told me she was his homey and there was nothing else to it. He said they have been friends for many years and he was not telling her she could not stay at his pad if she needed a place to stay. I am not sure how to handle this. I know he has a lot of female friends he calls homies, but I feel things are different with this woman.

Response:

It is really hard to tell if it's only friendship or something more. If the two of you have a trusting and honest relationship, then this woman shouldn't be a threat to your relationship with him. On the other hand, if he is not being sensitive to your feelings, and is not considering how you feel about this at all, then maybe you should tell him that if she is a friend, she would understand if he told her about how you felt.

Tell him that a true friend would not insist on imposing if it would make his girlfriend uncomfortable. If he insists after you bring this to his attention, then all you can do is to observe their relationship. If you're included in their activities, then most likely she is just a homey. If you are not, then maybe it is more than what he says it is. This is something you'll have to wait to see. Good luck.

Situation

36 You Never Know Where You Stand

What is wrong with these men today? You can't trust anything they say. One day they say this, and the next day they say that. It's like you never really know where you stand. This guy has been calling me for at least six months now. He's out of town a lot on business. I assume he is telling the truth because he only calls me once a month and the rest of the time I can't reach him.

Now, I did catch him in a lie once. He said he was out of town just last week and then he said he did something that I know was right in town last week. I know he does work a lot because he has a beautiful home, car, and he is a great dresser. He has money in his pockets too. When we do go out, it is always to a nice restaurant, and we have a great time.

But what's puzzling me is that he hasn't really advanced on me in a sexual way. First, I thought it was because he was being a gentleman, but recently he mentioned he is in a long-term relationship and he doesn't want to do anything. I don't get it. I don't know how to take this one. See, he came at me, so what does he want from me? And if he is in a relationship, why the hell is he at me at all?

Response:

That does seem a bit confusing . Maybe he is in a monog-amous relationship, but it could be lacking something he needs in his life now. At this point you really can't tell what he is doing. Sometimes men just need a friend. This sounds strange because we think men only need male friends. There are some men who need and value female friends, and he might just like your company.

Another possibility is that he could be a man in a relationship with many women. Remember the lie you caught him in; no matter how you look at it, it is still a lie. See, you really don't know where you stand with this guy. I would say maybe it's a good thing the two of you have not gone any further than friendship at this point. You may not want to be involved that way with him if he is in a relationship already and it means so much to him that he won't make any moves on you. Looking at things objectively and assuming he is telling the truth about his woman, his actions are to be admired. Nice dinners and good conversations are never a bad thing. Relax and Enjoy!

There are still good men out there, even if he is just your friend.

Situation

37 He is a Horoscope Dater

Well, I went to dinner with the world's number one horoscope dater. We sat at this beautiful French restaurant enjoying the red wine and the quiet and quaint ambiance. Nothing prepared me for two hours of all about the zodiac signs. This man talked only and completely about the different zodiac signs of the women he has dated. It went from how to approach them, how to deal with them, and how certain women of the zodiac like certain things. It Was Gross Really.

When I realized he was not going to get off the zodiac thing, I asked him about my sign. This fool point blank said, "Oh, we don't get along." He said my sign was too needy for a strong sign like his. He is an Aires, and I am a Cancer. If this statement wasn't the turn-off of all turnoffs, then sitting there the whole two hours was.

Except for the dinner, the drinks, and the beautiful surroundings, I should say no if he asks me out again. I don't know if I should ever give him another date or just mail him another astrology book. He was doing great with the beautiful restaurant and all; then as he drank and got drunker, the Zodiac-lover thing got longer and in more graphic detail. How can someone make something so beautiful turn out so ugly? Well, if you don't know, ask the horoscope dater. Yuck.

Response:

What a price to pay for a great dinner, drinks, an atmosphere. I don't think anyone would envy you at this point. I really don't blame you for not wanting to go out with him ever again. This probably felt like you were stuck in a nightmare or something for two hours. All I can say is, follow your first mind. If you feel not to go out with him again, then maybe you should not. On the other hand, maybe he just had a little too much to drink and was under some stress. But let's hope that this is not how he handles stress, by drinking.

It will be up to you to decide if you want to take that chance of another date with him. If there were other things about him that you admired, then maybe one more date will give you a clearer picture of him. Maybe he is not as superficial as he came off to be on this date; maybe you should get to know him a little better, and having one more date with him will let you know what you are truly dealing with. If he comes off the same then you know what he is. "A Big Fat Loser." If you find that he is not like that then maybe he was having an off night then maybe you can give him one more date. It will be on this date that you will be able to see if there is a pattern or not. You decide if he is worth all the trouble.

Situation

38 He Was Not Romantic At All

I know he's a good guy, and I know he cares about me, but it's just that he doesn't know what to do, ever, about anything. He is not romantic in any way. I'm the one who has to show all of the affection in this relationship. I set up everything for us, from arranging our dates together to getting tickets for concerts we may want to go to.

I have to choose where we go to eat; I have to choose everything. I thought it was because he didn't make a lot of money, so he was shy about taking the lead in the romance department. But now he has a much better job and makes a lot more money. Still nothing has changed; he still is not romantic and shows no initiative in this relationship. I don't know how to make him do more for our relationship.

Response:

Some men have never been taught how to be romantic, and some men think it is for the woman to do everything in the romance area of the relationship. Whatever his reasons are, you will never really know unless you ask him why he is not more romantic in this relationship.

This needs to be discussed if it bothers you. Maybe if he knew how you felt, he would try to do better. Tell him how you feel, and he may try and be more romantic for you. If nothing changes, then maybe he is showing you it's not what he cares to do for you or the relationship. If this is not enough for you or you're not satisfied with his behavior, then more serious discussions about your relationship need to take place.

Remember, people don't change unless they want to. If he doesn't want to do more, then you will either have to settle for less than you want, or settle for someone else who is more romantic. I really hope the two of you can work it out and have many romantic times together for many years to come.

Situation

39 I Have Not Told Anyone

My man and I had this terrible fight last night. It started out small, but the things he said to me make me think about my life and my childhood. He said that I always bring in my insecurities whenever I can't reach him by phone. He told me he was sick and tired of trying to fight an uphill battle, and that he can't win no matter what he does to make things work with us.

He believes there must be something that happened to me when I was a child because I can't find peace within. This really did hurt me because he doesn't know about any abuse that I may have encountered when I was a child. I did go through abuse.

I did have very bad experiences; my teenage boy cousins used to expose themselves to me. I was only four years old, but I never forgot this. I have not told anyone until now. Maybe my man is right; maybe I need to deal with this so I can get myself straight.

Response:

I do believe that is right: if something this traumatic has happened to you as a child, then you might need to really deal with this before you can be at peace with yourself. Holding something like this in for all these years may have affected you in certain ways. There probably is pain and anger deep down inside of you.

Professional help may be needed to clear your mind of some of these things. Many things that may happen in your life as an adult may not be entirely your fault because some things may be a result of what happened when you were only four years old. But now that you are an adult, it is your responsibility to get things straight and seek help if you need it. I really hope you get the help needed so you can have a beautiful and loving relationship with yourself and your partner in the future.

Situation

40 He Is Her Caretaker

I fell in love with this young man, and he fell in love with me. His aunt who raised him became terminally ill with cancer. He moved into her home to be her caretaker. When we met, he was totally consumed with taking care of her. He was working at home and he didn't have a lot of time for our relationship.

I am a career woman, and I sometimes have to go out of town for business, I am very busy. My younger man worries that I will meet someone who is more prominent than he is. He drives me crazy with his jealousy. He calls me all day just to hear my voice and sense what I am doing. When I am busy and cannot answer the phone when he calls, he goes crazy.

I am flattered, and at the same time his behavior is worrisome. Lately he has become revengeful. He talks about his ex-girlfriend coming by to bring him food and visit with his aunt. At first I thought it was harmless. But recently I have suspicions that they are seeing each other again. I have been faithful to him. But he doubts me. He says things like he's intimidated by my maturity and he fears one day someone older and more successful than he is will take me away from him. He says he needs me near him almost always. He is 28 years old and I am 36. I believe we can have a wonderful relationship, but he is slowly killing it.

Response:

He is old enough to feel secure with you. But if he is that insecure for whatever reason and needs to have another woman on the side for his own security or to make you jealous, this relationship will never work. Keep this in mind: if you are a career woman, you don't have time to baby-sit your younger man.

The both of you will have to decide if this relationship is right for the two of you at this time in both your lives. It looks like two people headed in different directions. I say this because you need to be out of town for your business, and he needs someone right there with him all the time to make him feel secure. How can the two of you be happy like this if it doesn't change?

Situation

41 He Won't Ask If I'm Married, Is He?

I met this doctor at a convention. He is very handsome. I think he's married, but he has not mentioned it. I find it a little odd that he has not asked me if I am married or single. We have talked on the phone a few times. There have been plenty of times he could have asked me this question. I hesitated to ask him this question because at this point I am not sure if he would tell me the truth or not.

I didn't know where he was coming from, but around the fourth phone call he invited me to a convention he was going to in Hawaii. He wanted me to be his guest.

Everything about this man was absolutely perfect, at least the picture he painted was. I responded to his request by saying I would be busy that weekend. I chose to leave him alone at this point. It felt like this could be a married man's booty call, and I was not going to be the booty he calls for on his trip to Hawaii or his trip to anywhere else.

When he got back from Hawaii last week, he called me again. I asked him how his trip was, and he said it was great. Our conversation went as usual with him not saying much and me not asking much. I did say I wouldn't be talking to him much in the future because I was going to be very busy. He said fine, but he still continues to call although I don't answer his calls.

Response:
Maybe he is in a relationship of some kind, or maybe he

is really married. It sounds like a creeping man to me also. It does seem strange for him not to ask if you are single or not. It also seems strange that he would not bring up the subject. But to ask you to go away with him to Hawaii does sound like he had the booty call thing in mind.

You did the right thing by leaving this one alone. I would have asked him if he was married so that I could get some closure on this matter. But you chose not to for whatever reason, and that's O.K. too. You did the best thing by cutting him off because why build a relationship with someone and not know where you are standing from the start?

Who knows; maybe he does this with other women. Maybe he is just a married Casanova. Be glad you are free of this elusive man. He could be a doctor, lawyer, or an Indian chief; if what he has to offer is not honest, then he's not offering much at all to anyone.

Situation

42 The Really Nice Guy I've Got

I am dating a really nice guy, and my mom and sister really like him. He is different from the guys that I usually go out with. I like the bad-boy type, the type that just don't give a s#*t about anything, and for some reason they are sexy to me. This guy I'm dating is such a gentleman: he opens doors for me, and he calls on time. He treats me with respect. He's got a very good job, and a very nice home, and a new car.

I know I should not be complaining, but although he is a good guy, I am not all that turned on to him sexually. I really don't want to lose him, but I have to have my bad boy on the side. It's like I want my bad boy for sex, and I want my good guy for everything else. I feel really bad about being this way and doing this to him because he really doesn't deserve this. I can't help myself. If I only had the good guy in my life, then my life would be like having steak without the seasoning, BLAND. If I only had my bad boy in my life, my life would be Sex, Sex, Sex, which ain't bad, but I would have nothing else.

I am in a dilemma because I am not ready to give up my bad boy and if my boyfriend (the good guy) finds out about my double life, I couldn't bear to lose him either. I'm afraid my boyfriend will find out, especially at the rate I'm going. Life would be so perfect if I can keep both, and my life could stay just the way it is.

Response:

You must first be honest with yourself before you can be honest with someone else. You must really decide what it is that you want in a relationship. Put your priorities in order; then you can take an honest look at your life. Start out by asking yourself is sex more important or is being treated well more important? This way you can answer the question for yourself, Are you ready for a good man? Maybe you will realize you are not ready for a serious relationship at this time in your life. Maybe you still need to search for someone who can fulfill you sexually and treat you like a lady as well.

It seems like this problem has nothing to do with the two men in your life. Each man is being himself. The good guy is being good, and the bad boy is being a good bad boy. The questions you need to address are who are you? and, What do you really want? When you do find a really good man, you must try to be ready for him because a good man is truly hard to find these days.

Situation

43 He Makes Me Become Someone I'm Not

These men can make you become someone you don't want to be. I want to be the type who has one man. I don't want to play at all of these mind games, and most of these games are so unnecessary. Your relationship could be going just great, and then you try to call your man, and he cannot be reached for hours. You leave a nice message like "Please call me back." You get no call back that day. Then the next day around midmorning you get the call from your man.

Here we go with the excuses as to why he never got your message yesterday afternoon. He left his charger somewhere at a friend's house. He was at the casino all night. His aunt or sister or friend got sick and he had to stay with them at the hospital all night. And he just got back home. I bet he just got back home and not from any of these places.

When you don't hear back from them you think of all kinds of things. You become suspicious of your man, and when this goes on several times a month, you assume it's another woman. This behavior makes a girl want to have a safety net, if you know what I mean.

So you start talking to other people, and this is what I mean when I say they make me become someone I am not. I don't want to talk to anyone else but him. But I don't want to be played, and I don't want to be left high and dry one day either if he is talking to someone else now.

Response:

I understand what you mean about being left high and dry one day. Not saying that this will happen, but his behavior does leave room for suspicion. Don't let a man change who you are just because he is not willing to do the right thing. Be who you are and look for a man who will be there for you. He may not be the right man for you and you may have to change your man to one that loves being your man and no one else's.

If your man is being or doing things you don't understand, then I assume he is not being straight with you. There is too much in life one has to do, and chasing a man who doesn't care about you or your feelings is not one of them. Therefore, chasing after someone who's playing games is more than a waste of time-it can become a waste of life, yours in particular. Don't waste your time or your life on someone who could care less by showing you careless behavior.

Situation

44 He Still has Feelings for Her

I have been living with this guy for six months. I work and support my six-year-old daughter and myself. He has a son two years old and a daughter thirteen. Both of his children live with their mothers. I have been noticing something he does with his son's mother. They just separated a year ago.

Every time we go out, he drives past her home. If we come back late at night, he will drive past her house. He doesn't think I notice what he's doing because he always takes different routes. One day we were driving past her house, and he became so upset he could not hold it. He said, "She's with that thug again, and I hate that."

He had seen this man's car in her driveway. She is dating a younger man now and that is driving him crazy. My man is 40 years old and his ex is 24 years old, and the man she is seeing now is 22 years old. My man went ballistic; he was arguing about it all the way home. When we got home, he called her house starting an argument with her on the phone. He was so angry.

When I asked him why he was so angry anyway, he kicked a chair clear across the room. He said, "Cause that's my girl." He was as shocked that he said that as I was. He has expressed to me that he didn't mean that and that he loves me. But this let me know he is not over his ex and he still loves her very much. His kicking the chair frightened my daughter and me.

I'm not sure if this is a true sign that he is violent or if it was a momentary thing. I have fallen in love with him. I wonder if time will make him stop loving her or at least stop caring so much? This hurts.

Response:

I agree with you that he may not be quite over with all of his feelings for his ex. He is still displaying jealousy over her, which shows he is still connected to her emotionally in some way. By his displaying jealousy over her relationship with the younger man, he shows there could be an issue with his age. He could feel rejected by her because he's 40 and she's 24, and she has a man now who is 22 years old, almost half his age.

The part that concerns me is kicking a chair across the room. This sounds like he has anger management problems. Before you get too deeply involved with him, you need to take a deeper look at this whole picture. There are some questions you really need to try and answer before you continue letting your love grow for this man. Does he have a violent streak? Does he have room enough in his heart for you on a deep level? Can he ever really let her go? These are just a few questions you really need to answer honestly.

It seems like he needs some serious time to deal with his feelings. He sounds a little confused about things and therefore has misplaced his anger. You must protect yourself in more ways than one. You must protect your little girl also. Maybe if the two of you give each other some space for a while you both can see things clearer. Think about giving each other a little space.

Situation

45 She Said, "Don't Let My Son Hurt You"

My fiancé and I just got engaged a month ago. We have been dating a year. He is successful and seems to love me very much. He does seem to be a little different in some ways, but I can't put my finger on it yet. I spoke to his mother one day when she called his apartment. She told me, "Don't let my son hurt you, OK, dear!" I said OK and I assumed she meant hurt my heart, like don't let him put other women in my face or something like that.

Now I am not sure what she meant after this happened to me. One day my fiancé and I got into an argument. He came over to me and grabbed my arm and twisted it behind my back. I couldn't believe he was doing this. It felt as if my arm would pop off. He finally stopped, but the next day I left for the whole day. When I returned home that evening, the house was dark. When I turned on the light, in the middle of the living room floor was a piece of paper, and his ring that I gave him was on it. I read the note and it said, "I don't trust you; here is my ring." I was completely confused and devastated. I tried to call him, but his phone was turned off.

Then all of a sudden he popped out of the closet. He was hiding in the closet the whole time. You could imagine how shocked I was when I saw him. It was like being in a true nightmare, and I couldn't wait to wake up. I told him I would be right back, I left, went, and got the police to escort me back there. I picked up all of my things, got in my car, and left.

He is either crazy or has a wicked sense of humor, and I am not laughing. He is trying to get back with me. He is calling my mom and my whole family begging them to get me to talk to him. I really don't think I should give him another chance. He frightens me.

Response:

I really think you have just answered your own question. If he frightens you, then why would you go back to him? Women should remember to always follow their gut instinct. You said it felt like a nightmare. This was your instinct telling you it didn't feel right. Sometimes when we get away from the situation, we forget how painful or uncomfortable it felt.

Don't let distance and the fact that you miss the good things the two of you had together make you forget how frightened you were that night! During these times we can easily dismiss what's really going on here. This man is displaying some unstable tendencies. Remember, his own mother warned you not to let him hurt you. There must be some things in his past that she knows about him that you don't.

Take heed to your feelings; when you were in that situation you didn't feel safe. Maybe you really need to step back a while longer and analyze this whole thing before you go back and make a big mistake and the next time you can't get out of it.

He doesn't seem like he is a very safe person to be around.

Situation

46 Two Times a Mama's Boy

The guy I am seeing now is two times a mama's boy. I say this because not only is he close to his mother, but he has a sister 16 years older than he is, and he's so close to her, that she's like his mama too. It's like he really has two mothers. It is overwhelming for me as his girlfriend.

When we met, he told me he was the baby of the family. When I met his family, it seemed as if his mom was the strong personality type and his sister was a complete diva. His dad seemed like the quiet type. When I am around them, I feel invisible. I love my man, and he loves me, but his mom and sister control everything. If we stay together, I will never have this man to myself, I will always have to share him.

Response:

This can be a very difficult position for you as his girlfriend. This is not completely his fault; he was raised, this way by his mom and his sister. I can see what you mean by two-times a mama's boy, once with his mother and the other with his sister because she is so much older. I seriously feel he may need to learn how to take his control from them.

His father is not an assertive man, so he did not set the example for him. Maybe your knowing how he was raised will help you to understand him better. The two of you can work through this if your man really wants to change. There won't be much of a change if you're the only one wanting him to change. He has to want this change also. Work with your man and not against his family, and I am sure things will work out for all of you.

Situation

47 We Played Strip Poker

e played strip poker last night. So a few of my friends came over; there were four couples. We all have been friends for about two years now. We do everything together, go on vacations together and spend holidays together. But this is the first time we have ever played this game together.

We all got so drunk from shots of tequila that my very best girlfriend dared my man to show her his thing, and before I could get up and snatch his ass or hers, he had it out for all to see. I know we were all drinking, but don't you think they both went too far? She is definitely a very ex-best friend of mine now. I still can't believe my man did this. I really don't know what to make of this. I know we all were drunk or close to it, but this is a little too much for me.

Well, at this point I am not speaking to either one of those fools. In one split second my relationship with my man and my best friend has changed forever. I now question my best friend and my man.

Response:

I do understand how you feel, and something like this is definitely not to be taken lightly. But, remember, you all were pretty loaded, and if you guys decide to play strip poker, what exactly do you think that means? I always thought it meant stripping at some point. I do know you did not expect this to happen, but it did.

It could've been just one of those impulsive moments. Let's just say as long as the two of you are together, nothing may happen. But if the two of you breakup and there's some interest between the two of them, well, who knows?

Playing games like strip poker, or let's switch partners, or anything like that is very dangerous between friends. There may always be someone who wants someone else in the group. They are waiting in the wings in case something goes wrong with someone's relationship. The one waiting in the wings will always be available to snatch up that lonely person, who they have been wanting for. All you can really do now is be aware that there are some questionable feelings between the two of them, so keep your eyes open and never play strip poker with them again.

Situation

48 My Boyfriend has a Revolving Head

Whenever I'm with my new boyfriend, he shows me undivided attention, but when we are in public, he has a revolving head.

He looks at every attractive woman passing; this is while we are walking together. I was shocked at his behavior when he first did this; I told him I did not like it, but that has not stopped him. How should I deal with this problem without looking jealous and, most of all seeming insecure. I am really into this man, and he says he's into me too. So what is this thing that he's doing?

Response:

Well, you can start looking at attractive men too, but that is not really the solution. You want this man to show you respect and not do such a thing. Even if he stops when the two of you are together, unless he understands what this relationship means to you and unless it means something to him, there is no guarantee this behavior will stop.

Maybe it's time the two of you sit down and redefine this relationship. It's better to know what each of you wants out of the relationship now than to continue like this, which will develop insecurities and major mistrust in the future.

Situation

49 This Creep Brings Her to Church

I had been dating my boyfriend for four years, but in the last year we have been on-again off-again. He claimed he still wanted to make our relationship work. So I kept trying with him. But the whole time I was trying to make it work, he was securing for himself another relationship.

I didn't pick up on the signs. I kept on dismissing them by making excuses to myself for his behavior. I would say, that is just the way he is. I started to accept him not doing the small things for me that I know a man should do, simple things like opening up a door for me. I had not realized that our relationship was over until he showed up in church with another woman.

He brought her to the same church we have been going to for two years. He did this in front of all of my friends. Needless to say, I was shocked and humiliated at the same time. As I was sitting there, I asked God why this creep did this to me in church. To my amazement, I was very calm. I do believe it was only the grace of God that allowed me to walk out of there as a lady.

I never said anything to him or to her. When service was over, I saw him open the car door so she could get in. The only words that were ringing in my head at that moment were, I am experiencing my ultimate hurt.

I kept saying this over and over. I knew this was our end; it was finally over between us. I knew this was the beginning of a new me. Through the hurt and pain, somewhere inside, I knew God was blessing me. I believe God wanted him out of my life for good. It was God's way of telling me there must be someone much better out there for me.

Believe me after this bazaar show my boyfriend gave the whole congregation, he is definitely out of my life, my mind, and my heart forever.

Response:

That was very nasty and cruel of him to bring another woman to church. I can imagine how you must have felt seeing him bring this woman to the same church the two of you have gone to for two years together. He used your love and compassionate heart to his total advantage. Just remember that it was in church that he chose to display his ugly behavior, and God is not asleep. God loves you, and he will keep you strong through this painful time. As you said, this was God's way of removing him from your life forever. God has a better path for you. I must say the way you handled the whole thing in church is to be commended. You remained a lady, and I know this was hard to do. But I must say truly God's Grace was on you that day for it held you together.

Remember, a person who is as cold as he is will not be as successful or happy in the long run. There's an old saying, "You reap what you sow." Keep the faith that God has a much better man for you. Believe this because God will not let you down. When you meet him, you must let me know because you will meet the right man, who is just for you. STAY BEAUTIFUL, STRONG, and SWEET, and may God continue his blessings upon you.

Situation

50 Photographer Introduces This B*#*h to My Man

My man and I are in a committed relationship. We have been living together for two years. We have a child together, and we're trying to make it work. A male friend of mine, who is a photographer, invited us out to this club. He was on an assignment to take pictures for the club's owner.

When we arrived, he was there already and he told us he wanted us to meet an old friend of his. It was this woman who is trying to become a model or something; come to find out she was 10 years older than my man and 15 years older than me. I am 28 years old, so she is 43 years old.

I didn't think much of the introduction although she stared at my man, and he stared back at her. At this point I became uncomfortable standing there. I believe this was the first time they had met, but I really don't know. So my man and I sat down and ordered drinks; the woman and my friend the photographer went to the back of the club. Ten minutes later my man said he would be back, and he went to the back of the club. Well about an hour or so past, and I went to the back to see what was going on, and he was sitting in a corner with this same woman we met earlier. I do believe more than conversation was taking place.

I have come to find out that she is a known ho and freak, and when it was necessary she has F#*ked not only men but women also to benefit her so-called career. It has been six months, and I believe my man is messing with this nasty b*#*h. I don't know if I should accuse him because he is such a liar and he wouldn't tell me the truth anyway. What bothers me is that he has been saying things like, "If we break up, I'm taking our son." I am an angry, frightened mess.

Response:

Because you are not getting honesty from this man, it makes this a difficult situation. He may be deliberately keeping you in the dark, especially if there is something going on with this woman and him.

If he has falling in love with this woman, you may have to evaluate things for yourself. All you can do at this point is watch and see what's going on for yourself. If you cannot get the truth out of him, then you will have to decide what you are going to do on your own. Either you leave the relationship or fight like hell to keep it. This is a decision you will have to make. If they want to be together, then there isn't much you can do. If this is the case then you need to take care of yourself and your child, and make sure if he does leave you, he doesn't take your child from you.

When you are dealing with a deceptive, selfish man like he seems to be, you must watch him closely. These types of men are very dangerous to women because they plan to do things that will hurt and destroy you long before you ever know what's going on. Beware.

Situation

51 His Quadruple Marriage Thing

A man I have been seeing for awhile just told me some devastating news. He told me that he was involved in a strange family-type relationship. He told me there were three people involved at the time, and the family always wants four people at a time.

He went on to explain how great this arrangement was for everyone involved. He said if one person has money, all have money. If one person succeeds, all will succeed. If one person fails, the others will be there to help them. This was their family pact, and this was his marriage.

This crazy fool asked me if I would become their fourth person. After expressing my very clear point of view, which was that I thought this was absolutely crazy and, no, I would not be part of this bizarre, crazy marriage thing, he continued. He wanted me to hear about it all before I jumped to a conclusion. He wanted me to know that like any marriage, it must be consummated, which meant all four of the people would have to have sex together. To put it more directly, each person must have sex with each person in the family. This was disgusting to me beyond belief, and I let him know exactly how I felt about it.

I have not seen this person since he told me this, and that was about six weeks ago. He just called me again yesterday. I have not returned his call, and I don't think that I will. The message he left on my voicemail was about us staying friends. I once thought of him as quite intelligent, but knowing this about him has totally changed my feelings and beliefs about him and his crew. I know that even friendship, could never work. Although he is very sexy, I have lost sexual interest in him completely.

Response:

I don't even think it would be to your benefit to keep him as a friend or anything else. So not returning his call would be a good thing for you to do. A person believing in something like this raises many questions. First of all, what is in his past that would allow him to think something like this is just fine?

There must be bisexuality, insecurity, inferiority, and just plain freakism among other complex mind problems here. If you did decide to remain friends with him, I'm sure it would be a difficult friendship to maintain. If your feelings have changed toward him, and you're no longer interested, then why waste your time?

In my opinion, this could never be a normal relationship of any kind. If I were you, I would let this one get away, but I am not you. Think hard before you continue in this maze of madness.

Situation

52 I Don't Want an Exclusive Relationship

I am involved with a younger man. I could be his mother if I had him when I was in my early teens. We started out as only friends. He would ask my opinion about what he should do at work if he had problems on his job. He would even talk to me about his girlfriends. After a few months of talking, he started to drop hints like he wished he could be with me.

It was flattering at first, but his conversations grew more serious. We spoke for over a year; within that year he made constant advances toward me. I simply told him maybe we should do something and get it out of the way. I was really joking with him, but he didn't see any thing to joke about.

He took me up on this, and a few months later he and I became lovers. I've got my own life going, and he has his. I told him I don't want an exclusive relationship with him. I told him we were supposed to have sex just to get it out of the way. I thought we both understood this quite well. Now he's telling me he's falling in love with me. I have other people in my life who have been there for years. I don't want them to leave out of my life. This young man has expressed to me that he wants us to be together. I have great fears with him or any younger man.

I have expressed this to him many times. I told him because he is so many years younger than I am, I fear him cheating on me with someone younger. He has told me many

times this will not happen. I told him this is something he just
can't guarantee. I told him I believe this will happen because
he may feel he's losing out by being with an older woman. I
also fear that if I give up everyone for him, then maybe in ten
years he may leave me.

I told him I don't have the time that he does if this
relationship doesn't work. I would rather keep him as my
friend and keep my other lovers. I will admit I do love him
too, but my fears are greater at this point than anything else.
I believe I am making the right choice by keeping him as my
friend only.

Response:

Just remember, in all relationships chances must be taken
and in all relationships nothing is ever guaranteed. You can
be bigger than your fears and take a chance with your
younger man, or you could lose out on what could be a love
of a lifetime.

The other people in your life have been there for years,
and it has not developed into anything other than what it is
today. You could have more, or settle for mediocrity. It is
your life, and you know yourself better than I do. You will
have to decide if you could take that chance or not.

You brought up some good points on your behalf, and I
do see your point. If you could live your life without your
younger man being in your life exclusively, then I guess
that's fine for you. It seems as if your mind is made up
because you are so fearful of the future with him. Maybe it is
best for the two of you to remain close friends instead of
anything more. If nothing else, your fear alone will interfere
with the two of you having a really wonderful relationship.
Good luck on the decision you make. They say real love
comes once-in-a-lifetime, and that could be at any age.

Situation

53 Does He Care or Care Less?

I am so sick of being the one who loves him so much. How can he be so strong? He never gives in to calling me first or making any advances first. I have to be the one to call him, and if I want to see him, I have to make the first move.

He tells me he loves me and asks if I love him too. Usually after we get busy and have sex, he is very quiet, and then I just leave. I don't try to start any conversations with him because he is very moody, and we'll just start to argue. Then I won't hear from him again until I make the next call. He calls me back sometimes. I just think he is not a phone person. What do you think is going on with him? Do you think he'll soon come around?

Response:

A phone person or not, if a man is truly interested, he will make more contact with you than what you say he's doing. This doesn't sound like love to me. It doesn't even sound like deep "like." I know what I am saying is not what you want to hear, but you need to hear it anyway. I Don't Think He Is Very Interested.

He may be telling you he loves you, and that might be part of the act he's playing on you. It's not about his strength; it's about his interest. When a man is not that interested in a woman, his not calling can appear as strength, if that's what you want to call it. But what it's called is lack of interest. If his heart is not there, a man is not going to call you or chase you down.

When a man is interested or in love with a woman, he doesn't act this way at all. A man in love will chase, run, jump, or do whatever it takes within legal reason to get the object of his affection in his arms forever. It isn't a matter of coming around either. This may be as much coming around as he'll ever do. If you are waiting for a change, you might be wasting precious time on someone who could care less. Just look at his actions. They will tell you the truth.

Situation

54 My Stepmother and My Ex

M y pig-ass stepmother, who raised me, can't accept getting old. She is 56 years old, and I'm 22. She still tries to compete with me. She has two sons and no daughters of her own. She has a son, 19, and she and my dad had my little brother, who is now 12 years ago.

My dad never really saw it, but she has always been in some kind of competition thing with me. Every boyfriend I've ever had told me of her flirtatious statements to them. I have tried to ignore her doing this, hoping it would stop. But it has really gone too far now.

I was dating a rapper, but last year we broke up. Recently, friends of mine told me some disturbing news. I was told that my stepmother went out to visit my ex-rapper boyfriend while he was on tour in another state. She didn't just go to see him in concert; she went out there to party with him.

The news came back to me that my stepmother is a real freak. I was truly devastated to find this out, and I was shocked that my ex-boyfriend would do such a thing to me. I know my pig-ass stepmother is very capable of doing such a thing. I am in a dilemma because if I tell my dad, it will break his heart. It may even break up the family and my little brother will truly be destroyed also. What should I do? And how can I react anywhere near normal around her again? I Hate her.

Response:

I can see your dilemma. You now know the truth about your stepmother. Her being your little brother's mother and your father's wife does put you in a very strange place among them. The thought of having to deal with your stepmother and your ex-boyfriend betraying you I'm sure is a lot.

The two of them probably thought no one would ever find out. But everyone did. Who knows, maybe this has been going on for a long time. Maybe she's done this with other boyfriends of yours. You may never know. Now you will have to decide whether you will tell your father or not. You say you are concerned that if you tell your father it will not only hurt him but it could destroy the family. Well, it doesn't seem like your stepmother cared if her family would be destroyed.

With her doing such things, the family is already destroyed. Maybe your father knows what type of woman she is and has chosen to look the other way. Then again, maybe he just thinks she doesn't mean anything when she is flirting with other men. She probably thinks she has gotten away with this.

In any case, I am sure you feel very upset for many reasons. I don't know if you could hold something like this back from your father. If it becomes too much for you to deal with, maybe you will have to talk to someone. I'm hoping you make the right decision for yourself so that this very irresponsible behavior by your stepmother and your ex-boyfriend doesn't become your burden, but it's now your nightmare. Just remember to do the right thing for you now.

Situation

55 This So-Called Friend of Mine

I have a friend; well, I thought she was a friend anyway. I happen to meet this woman who was attending this music-listening party; she is about 12 years older than I am, so I respected her like a mentor, and we became friends.

She was an assistant to a couple of people in singing groups. My singing career is just getting started, and so she became my assistant also. Every time we would meet someone new, she would take their number and take care of any business appointments that would follow.

When these people would call to speak with me, she would block them by telling them that I was not interested in what they had to say. After telling them this, she would then say she should meet with them without my knowing; that way she could influence me to listen to them. Most of them went along with this, and after meeting with them she would propose having sex with them.

I found out about this horrendous behavior from a man who didn't believe what he was hearing. She had called this man's office and disguised her voice saying she was me. She was behaving irrationally and arrogantly and making ridiculous demands and making sure they knew it was me that was on the phone.

This person found me and told me, "He didn't believe that ridiculous, rude person was me." He said when he met me I was such a beautiful person that there would be no way this buffoon he heard on his phone could be me. He believed that it was my assistant. I then told him, "It was definitely not me." Well it was my assistant because after that there were other people who also told me about some bizarre things she had said on the phone to them, and all the while claiming she was me.

I don't know how much damage she has done to my career and me but I have a great record deal now, and I am booked on tour for six months. Can you believe there are crazy people like this sabotaging people's lives and careers? I just wanted to get completely away from this nut. I didn't press charges or anything; I just wanted to move on with my life and my career. I feel she has taken enough from me already, especially my time and my energy. All I said was good riddance forever. But I do hope she gets caught in a big way one day.

Response:

You should be grateful that the person told you what she was doing to you because if you didn't find out when you did, so much more damage could have been done to you.

I don't blame you for wanting to get away from her as quickly and as soon as you could. It is obvious that this person is not stable mentally or she is an outright criminal who steals people's identity.

Now, that witch is very lucky you are a cool-headed person and didn't kick her crazy want-a-be-somebody Ass. Let's just say, with behavior like that, it's just a matter of time when trouble will come a knocking at her door.

Well, continued success in your career, and in endeavors you decide to go into, and I would strongly advise you to handle your own business from now on. But no more secretaries, please.

Situation

56 We're Broken Up, but I Still Let Him Sex Me

I have been dating my boyfriend for three years. We sort of broke up a few months ago, but we still have sex on occasion. When we were together, we practiced monogamy. At least this is what I did. We haven't seen each other in a few weeks. When we talked on the phone, he told me he was dating but nothing serious.

When he said nothing serious, I took it as meaning he wasn't thinking of them as special. I know when we first dated we used condoms for the first six months. After the six months, we never used condoms. We believed neither one of us would dare have unprotected sex with each other if there was a possibility that either one of us had anything.

This was our code of ethics. When I recently had sex with him, he wanted to have sex just like before we broke up without the condom. I gave into his way but I am deeply concerned about the next time. I am not sure if he is having unprotected sex with the other women. But if he is, and he is not protecting himself, then I will never really know; see this is a problem for me.

Response:

Yes, this is a problem for you. He lets you know that he is with other women, and, of course, there could be a chance that he is not wearing condoms with them. Don't be naïve, but my first question to you would be why are you still having sex with a man that is no longer your boyfriend? If you say because you can't get over his sex, then I will say to you that you must get unwipped. It is obvious that you are sprung on this man. Why would you want to continue with an ex-boyfriend who is clearly through with the relationship other than sex?

It seems like you have some self-esteem issues to deal with if you accept this nonsense from him. If a man who was once your man and had no other woman but you becomes an ex and now has lots of women and tells you about them, he is showing he has no respect for you at all.

You have shown him how to treat you, and that is with no respect. He treats you this way because you are showing no respect for yourself by continuing to have sex with him after the two of you have broken up-and without a condom. The man tells you of his other women, and you continue to have sex with him without a condom. If you can't leave him, then show dignity for yourself by insisting that he wears a condom when he is having sex with you. Please look at what is really going on here, and try and move on. I am sure you can find a good man that will show you love, respect, and have great sex too. But you will have to unhook from this one. Think about it. Think about your self-respect.

Situation

57 He Didn't Have Gas Money To Give Me

I couldn't believe he didn't have gas money to give me. I have been seeing this guy a few weeks now. This particular night it was raining, and I mean it was pouring down rain. It was about 11:00 at night and he promised to come over my house this night. I was expecting him, so I did not go to sleep. He finally called me; he was about an hour late when he called.

When he called, he said he needed a ride to my house asked if I would come and get him. I really wanted to see him, so I went. I told him that I would need gas money, and he said sure. When I got there and asked for the gas money, he said he would have to owe it to me for the next time. But what got me was his nonchalant attitude about it. I was furious and felt lied to.

I would not have felt so badly about him not having gas money to give me if he had just come out and told me before I got there. But I guess he thought I wouldn't come and get him. But what if I really needed it to get back home? We both would be stuck out there looking stupid.

This was one night I felt more than used. I said after this night I will never pick him up again anywhere, and I mean that. I was so mad at his ass, that if I didn't want to have sex so bad that night, I would have left him standing in that rain after he said he didn't have the money. More than the money, it's the principle of the thing to me. Am I making too much of this or what?

Response:

I'm glad to hear that you will not be picking him up anywhere anymore. If his behavior was that nonchalant, then I see your point. This sounds like something he has done before. Maybe other women have picked him up from wherever at unreasonable hours in the night before. Maybe no one has ever asked him for gas money before either. He also sounds like a spoiled one. Some women may feel it's embarrassing for them to ask for the gas money, but remember he's not embarrassed to ask you to pick him up.

So I am proud that you did ask him for the money. Even more embarrassing for him is that he didn't have the money to give to you when you got there. This should be a good lesson to start from. If the man wants to see you, the least he can do is get to you on his own.

Even though you may have wanted to see him badly, you should not have gone to pick him up, especially at that hour of the evening and in the pouring rain. Maybe that was his way of testing you to see how far you would go for him in more ways than one. Your actions showed you were desperate.

A man will look at your actions and come to the conclusion that you are a desperate woman and can't do without him. If these are the kinds of messages we women are sending men, then why should these men worry about having a car and, least of all, having the gas money to give back to us when we get there. When women make things too easy for men, they become spoiled and hard to deal with. If we want men to treat us right we first must raise our standards and don't let them take advantage of us. There are ways to treat a man well without lowering ourselves. I am not bashing men; I'm just telling it like it is.

Situation

58 Yes, It Was Rape

I went over to his house because he invited me. We have not
seen each other for two weeks, and we have been arguing
on the telephone this whole time.

This is normal for us, but we usually make up. So I go to
his house and he lets me in. He was strange to me on this
night.

His attitude with me was different, and he wasn't talking
much, which was very strange to me also. I said to him, "I'm
not going to stay tonight." But this didn't sit well with him.
I started to put my jacket on, when he grabbed me. I said,
"I'm going to go." He walked up and pushed me down on the
floor, and he proceeded to have sex with me. No matter how
hard I fought him he continued. The truth is, he raped me. My
boyfriend who I love raped me.

He said nothing when it was over. I was devastated, and
I couldn't believe what just happened. I left without saying a
word. I didn't know what to say; I was in shock. I kept
thinking, well, he is my boyfriend so how can it be rape? I am
so confused and hurt, sad, and disappointed in him. I feel
really lost and violated now.

Response:

Anytime someone proceeds to have sex with you when
you have clearly said, "No," it is called "Rape." Whether it is
from a boyfriend or not, it is still rape. Now you must decide
how you are going to handle this serious matter. Rape is a

violent act. Rape is stealing something very precious from someone. It's something that is hard to replace, and that is your self dignity.

Though you may have had nothing to do with him raping you, women somehow are left to feel they are to blame for this terrible act of violence. They feel blame maybe because it's through sex that this crime is committed, and woman blame themselves for a lot in the area of sex.

I don't advise you to accept this crime of violence just because you knew him or because he is your boyfriend. This could be the beginning of more serious offenses against you by this person whom you thought you knew. Seek help; secrets like these should never be held. But you must be safe from someone that can behave like this, and especially if it is someone you know and may see again.

Situation

59 I Will Show Up and Surprise His Butt

I have been told that my husband is cheating on me with a co-worker. Another of his co-workers, a female, called me and told me this. I believe this woman has also had an affair or a fling with my husband. To me she sounded like a woman scorned. This is why I feel she gave me the tip.

My husband is a road manager for this touring stage group. He goes out on tour for six weeks at a time. Every two weeks I go out to meet him in the city that they are performing in. I think I will surprise his butt and show up in a city he doesn't expect me to show up in. This way he won't be able to stage anything before I get there. Then I will be able to see what's what for myself.

I have always trusted my husband, but there is something a little different this time. There are a few young women on this tour, and I did get a hint that he is showing a lot of attention to one in particular.

The last time I went out to see them, I did notice one girl with long dreads; she grabbed my husband on his arm, and they were kind of joking around. He knew I was there looking at him, and when she whispered something in his ear, he looked straight at me as if he didn't want me to catch him or something. I really love my husband, and I know he loves me. But I will show up and surprise his butt.

Response:

If that's what you want to do, then do it; he is your husband. Wanting to see your husband at any time is just fine. But in the event you do confirm your suspicions, handle your business in a way that doesn't make you behave irrationally. I'm sure it would be very difficult to just keep a cool head if you were to see another woman in his arms or in his bed.

What I mean is, don't do something that will end you in a jail somewhere or get you physically hurt. Remember, what you have heard up until now is just suspicion. There is always another way to handle stuff like this. I call it "stuff" because you never know if the woman who called you and told you this is just a mess maker. What if she tried to make a pass at your man, and he turned her down or something? Sister girl would really be an upset woman, and as you said, she sounded like a woman scorned. You never know, so if I were you, I would take it slow and easy. I would go but I would not be on the attack. I would just be cool and just watch and especially watch Miss let-me-give-you-a-tip or hint or whatever she called herself doing to help you out.

Situation

60 She Has Control Over My Man

M y boyfriend and I are members of a church youth group. We are both 18 years old. The youth leader is a very attractive older woman; I think she is in her thirties. To me it seems like she has some sort of control over my man. He just does everything she says. She knows a lot of our secrets because she also counsels our youth group.

To me she seems like she uses her knowledge to control people for her benefit. I haven't told anyone about this but you. I would especially not tell the folks in church because they would think I'm losing it or something. The people at church think this woman can do no wrong. I know what I feel, and I know what I see. It's the way she deals with my boyfriend, which to me is more like a woman attracted to a man.

My boyfriend seems very flattered by all of her attention towards him. He says I'm reading too far into it, but I'm not if they're always together and she always has to go places with him for one reason or another. It is what I am looking at, and it is right there for me to see. In fact, it is right there for all to see. And this is embarrassing me. I really don't know what to do.

Response:

If your boyfriend is not relating exactly to you what is going on between the two of them, then there could be a problem. There really isn't any reason why he shouldn't tell you everything that is going on or not going on between the two of them.

Yes, your boyfriend should put you at ease in this situation. Maybe your boyfriend likes the attention because it makes him feel like he is a big deal around the people at church. The fact that she is showing him so much attention, for whatever reason, could be a problem. I can understand your feeling uncomfortable about this; if she knows that the two of you are dating, then, if her attention toward him is really innocent, why not include you in their activities?

Confront your boyfriend and just ask him point blank what is going on. If he doesn't give you an answer one way or the other, then become observant. I'm sure you'll get the right answer sooner or later. Continue participating in your youth group activities; I'm sure there are wonderful things to do with the group. If it turns out that more is going on with your boyfriend and the youth leader, then make your decision if you want to stay at that church or find another church home. You will see the truth because something like this can't hide forever.

Situation

61 It's Always About What I Do

very time my man and I have an argument, nothing is
ever his fault. The whole thing is always my fault. It
becomes constant blame on me for this or that. Instead
of letting it go, he holds on to it forever.

Out of the clear blue sky he will bring up something old.
He never lets it go. I feel bad because I always end up feeling
things are usually my fault. Deep inside I know it isn't. But
this is the way I feel about our relationship most of the time.

I am growing to hate being in a relationship where I feel
I am always wrong when I know it's not always my fault.
How do I stop feeling guilty for what I did not do?

Response:

First of all, take responsibility for what you do in this
relationship and not what he does. I have a question for you.
What are you afraid of? I ask you that question because it
seems as though you are afraid to stand up for yourself in this
situation with this man. If you are talking about a long-term
relationship with this man, then you need to really get a grip
on things now. The two of you both need to start acting like
adults and leave the kiddy stuff behind. What I mean by
saying to act like adults, I am saying take responsibility for
only what you do in the relationship, and he must do the
same. Boundaries really need to be set here because you
cannot control what he does or doesn't do therefore you need
not feel that you are responsible for anything he does or does

not do. This way what he does is on him, the same goes for what you do is on you.

If you are still feeling guilty after these boundaries are set, then you might want to look deeper into why you feel the guilt constantly. This relationship seems as though it will work if the two of you really want it to. Beware that he is not trying to control you with guilt. Looking a little bit deeper, there could be some other stuff going on too. Don't rule out the possibility that there could be some cover up to throw your mind into defense mode in order that you don't see something that he does not want you to see. The important thing for you to do is to find out why you are so guilty just because he blames you. Until you start to look deeper within yourself for the true reasons why you allow him to do this to you, it will continue – if not with him, with the next man you get involved with. Work on your stuff, get "you" straight first, and I believe things will fall into perspective for you.

Situation

62 I Fell In Love with His Phone Voice

I t was his phone voice that made me fall in love with him. I met this guy just as he was moving out of state. I met him one month, and the next month he was moving to another state. His job took him there. We talked to one another almost every night on the phone for two or three hours.

It was the things he would say and the way he would say them that got me. He is very intelligent and charming. He has qualities that I admire in a man. I do believe we were falling in love with each other. When I went down to visit him a few months later, in his new home state, it was as if he was a complete stranger to me. I knew him by his voice and not by who he really was.

It was a very weird thing to experience. Being face-to-face with him, he was like a stranger to me. I was in love with the voice of this man; it became so strange to me that I asked him to leave and go back to his house and call me from there. He did and I was OK talking to him again. I then realized that I was not in love with him at all but that I had fallen in love with this man's voice. It was as if his voice had a separate personality from him completely. When he and I were together, there was really no chemistry between us at all. We just didn't click. I have learned the importance of chemistry between two people. I have also learned that chemistry only takes place when two people are physically together.

Response:

That could happen if your relationship started on the phone first. A phone-chemistry and a phone-persona may develop. The phone persona comes from the person you imagine you are talking to because you really don't know this person any other way.

The conflict happens after you are in the person's presence and the phone persona is not who that person really is. It's not that the person lied to you or anything; it's what you imagined this person to be from his or her phone voice. It resembles a fantasy relationship where you can create the person you want behind the sound of his voice. Let's just say in the case of your friend his voice had more sex appeal and charisma than his whole body. Sometimes a person's voice can make you think less or more of them until you get to know that person better. I bet you never realized before this, the power of a person's voice.

I guess it can work the same way when you see someone who looks a certain way; it doesn't mean the person is that way. You have to get to know the person before you know who they really are. I guess this means always look further than what you see, and in your case look further than what you hear. All I can say is watch out for those sexy voices and talk to your men face-to-face.

Situation

63 His Male Lover Lives in France

I met this very handsome, sexy guy one summer night when I was coming out of a music concert. He likes the same music and different cultural things, like I do. We went out a few times, and he was the perfect gentleman.

One day at the end of the summer, he told me he was going to take a trip to France. He said he wanted to ask me something before he left. So we met for dinner, and he asked me to marry him. He gave me a beautiful diamond ring. My mouth dropped, I was elated and confused at the same time.

This was so weird to me because how could he ask me to marry him so soon, and without us ever really getting to know each other? We have only kissed. I'm only 19 years old, and I'm not ready for this yet. He knew I wanted to be married someday, and he wanted to marry someone someday too.

The look on my face made him ask me if I thought he was too old for me. He is 28 years old. I replied, "No, you are not too old for me; you're age is fine." I then asked him why he gave me this ring so soon; we only knew each other a few months. He said he knew from the first time he saw me that he wanted to marry me.

He then said, "I want to tell you something." He said, "Whether we make this our reality or not, this ring is yours." He grabbed my hand and said, "I really do love you and because I love you I want you to know something about me." He went on to say, "I have a male lover and that is why I'm going back to France."

Well, after the "male lover part," I guess my ears went deaf because everything else he said sounded muffled like I had cotton balls in my ears or something. I remember getting into a cab and looking back at him; everything from the cotton balls in my ear to the cab is an absolute blur. I have no idea what he said or what I said.

As I got into the cab and looked back at him, I knew it would be the last time I would ever see him again. I was numb for about a week; I guess I was in some sort of shock balloon or something. It's been six weeks since this happened. He got back from France a week ago, and he called me; he wants to talk. I felt he and I were the perfect couple up until that point. I do respect the fact that he told me, but I can't quite get over it or him. I think I fell in love with him. I want to reconnect with him but only as friends. I'm really not sure what to do.

Response:

I would say above all else he must care deeply for you too because he did tell you the truth. I would even say he did love you in his way. If there is love between the two of you, reconnecting with him could possibly be dangerous for you, if all you want to be at this point is a friend, then it could be dangerous emotionally for you because your feelings started in a certain way and to change them into friendship might not work out.

Maybe this relationship needs to be left alone for a while. It was a shock to you and things ended so abruptly, I would think you need some time to reevaluate all that is going on here. However I do think you need some sort of closure to what the two of you had before he told you he had a male lover. You will eventually find peace in this whole thing, but it will take time. So don't rush to any conclusions; just give yourself time and space from this person so that you can decide with a clear head what you want to do.

Until then get busy taking care of you! If this relationship is to be, then it will be because you decided that it should be and not because you were bamboozled into it.

Situation

64 My Lover's Daughter is My Age

He was an older gentleman I would say in his late 50s. We met when I was waiting for my plane. He said he just missed his. Then he said, "I guess it was suppose to be." We started to talk, and he asked me what was I studying for. I told him my real estate exam. Then he asked me my age; I told him I was 36 years old. He said, "I have a daughter 36 years old." Then I asked him his age. He smiled and didn't answer me.

I then said, " I guess you are about 65." He never said yes or no. He was very handsome, very intelligent, and a complete gentleman. I had to go catch my plane, so we exchanged numbers, and he called me the next day. I don't usually date men that much older than I am, but he was different. I think it was all that charisma.

After talking on the phone with him for a few months, I felt very comfortable with him. So I went to his city to visit with him. I felt so cared for and secure with this man. He told me even though he is 73 years old, he only dates younger women. I was amazed that he was that old, and he did not look it and he certainly didn't act it. Then I became curious about sex with him. I just had to know what it was like to have sex with someone that age. You would not believe what a great lover he is.

I don't know if he was a great lover when he was a young man, but he is a great lover now. Maybe that's how it goes: men become great lovers when they get older or something. All I know is he is going to be my best kept secret. I'll never let him go. I can't believe I got sprung over an old man; he was supposed to get sprung over me. Isn't that the way it goes? I know he has other women because he told me so, but it didn't bother me then.

I question him all the time about where he goes when I'm not around. What makes it worse is that his daughter is always introducing him to her friends. His daughter is my age and so are her friends. I told him I want him to be with only me, but he still sees other young women. How do I stop being jealous of other women being with him?

Response:

It does seem like you've met a real Casanova. If this is something he has done for years, maybe he will never stop. Maybe he knows that younger women may not take him seriously if he tells them he wants to be with them only, so he just deals like this. If you have told him that you want to be with him only and he still hasn't changed, then maybe the relationship is not as serious for him as it is for you.

Maybe in this case the relationship isn't about age; maybe it's about two people in a relationship. Just because he is older and you are so much younger than he is, doesn't guarantee that he is going to want to be with you. The same goes for the fact that just because he is older doesn't guarantee, you won't fall in love with him.

It seems that, for you, it's about the man and not about the novelty of being with a man his age. And, for him, you didn't show him how you were different from any of the rest. This man only deals with younger women so being different may have meant not showing how curious you were to have sex with him so soon. I'm sure this man has seen it all. It really would take someone special to get him to change. So, for now, if you don't intend on letting him go, try working on being more mysterious when it comes to this man. Just enjoy the time you do spend with your best -kept secret. This seems like a very interesting relationship, so just enjoy!

Situation

65 So He Likes Short, Tiny Women

My very fine male friend tells me I am just not his type. We've known each other for six months. He constantly tells me that I am not his type of female because he likes very tiny women. I am 5 ft. 6 in. tall and I weigh 146 lbs. I don't consider myself a very big woman. But he says he likes women who are 5 ft. tall and 100 lbs.

He is 6 ft. 2 in. tall and very thin. I think we fit perfectly together, and we get along great too. There is nothing I don't like about him. I felt in time he would see me the same way I see him, but no luck so far.

I just felt that he would eventually turn my way and it was just a matter of time. Last night I went over to his place unannounced and he let me in. When I went inside he was sitting on the sofa with a co-worker of his. His co-worker was a very handsome male. He introduced him to me and also mentioned he was married. It was so strange to me; they were playing chess, drinking, and playing mellow music. It was 12:30 a.m. Sunday morning. I felt very uncomfortable, so I didn't stay very long.

This looked like a very romantic setting to me. It was very puzzling. I am not sure what that was. As I think about it, I have never seen my friend with a woman other than me. He and I have never had anything more than friendship. I would hate to think what I'm thinking is true, but does this sound like a down-low thing going on? I need a second opinion.

Response:

You never really know by looking at it; maybe that is why it's called down-low. It's hard to see through it unless you have hard facts. I am not saying that your friend is a down-low brother, but if he is, they know how to keep it a puzzle to others.

These types of relationships are nebulous, deceitful, and quite disturbing to others looking on. In a relationship with a person you can't figure out, there is usually a reason behind it. Maybe you should not try to pursue anything more than simple friendship with him until you find out more of the truth about him. Maybe that's all that's there for you at this point, a really great friendship. So take it slow, find out more, and enjoy what you have.

Situation

66 The Red Flag of Relationships

He was text messaging me, and calling me, and saying cute things on the phone all the time. Then one day came the jealousy and possessiveness. We haven't been dating a long time, so his overbearing attitude towards me seems out of place. I am used to going and coming as I please. I have a lot of male friends, so when he told me that I will have to end my friendship with all of my male friends, I got upset.

I also had a picture of my ex on the wall, and he demanded that I take it down. I took it down, and he still was upset; he argued all that night and refused to have sex with me. I really care for him, but I hate that he's trying to change my lifestyle. I wonder if I give it more time if he will see that my friends are not a threat to him.

Response:

I hope you can see this behavior is a red flag. He seems as though he needs lots of reassuring. There seems to be some baggage from a prior relationship that he is bringing into this one. Unless you want to be his therapist or spend lots of time reassuring him, then maybe you should consider him to be one of your friends too.

Maybe the two of you need to get to know each other better before starting a relationship. Sometimes a relationship that could have worked never gets a chance because the two people just don't know each other well enough. Sometimes a person may say something a certain way, and unless you know the person, you may take what is said the wrong way. Something this simple can even end what could have been a beautiful and prosperous love affair.

If you give each other time to get to know one another, I'm sure he will see that your male friends are harmless. Otherwise, if he is that jealous and overbearing, you might be explaining every move you make. I would say look at the red flag of warning that he is waving in front of you, and if you take time to know him better, you will be able to see if this is his real personality or just a bundle of fear.

Situation

67 My Boyfriend is Attracted To His Cousin's Girlfriend

I went to my boyfriend's family reunion, and his male cousin and his cousin's girlfriend were there also. This is the second time my boyfriend and I met her. I am disturbed by something that I know I see but I can't say anything about it, at this point.

This is what is bothering me; see, my boyfriend kept talking to her every time I was not around. She is in a sorority, and my boyfriend is in a fraternity, so they have that in common. I am not in a sorority.

Every time his cousin or I was not in the room my boyfriend was at her, talking and asking questions, laughing, and every time I walked back into the room, they would end the conversation abruptly. I am very uncomfortable about this because it seems that my boyfriend is somewhat attracted to her. She is very pretty, and when I saw her, I knew my boyfriend would like her because she is his type also.

Response:

Well I don't know how your boyfriend and his cousin usually deal with each other's girls, but this does seem a little out of place. Maybe you need to tell your boyfriend how this makes you feel, and that it's very uncomfortable for you when he would start a conversation with this girl whenever you and his cousin would not be in the room. Let him know how you felt when the conversation would stop abruptly whenever you came back into the room.

There should be open conversation between them when you are around also. I am sure if there is no interest between the two of them, your boyfriend will change his behavior. If there is interest, the best you can do is let your boyfriend know you are aware of it. The right thing for your boyfriend to do after you let him know how you feel about this is to respect how you are feeling, and those private conversations should not continue.

I'm sure your boyfriend loves you and doesn't want to make you uncomfortable. It is a possibility that he doesn't mean any harm. So keep an open mind, and I'm sure it will work out fine. If it continues, then maybe he is showing you who he is, a flirt. I would say it is always better to find out sooner than later.

Situation

68 My Sneaky B*#*h Ass Sister

y sneaky b#@ch-ass sister strikes again. She comes to visit me for a few days, and I'm really glad she's here with me. We always have so much fun together, but there is a quality about her that I wish was not there. We are only 18 months apart, and everyone always thought we were twins growing up. This made life very fun, especially for me. It was like I was equal to my big sister.

We grew up in Louisiana, and there were some clubs we used to go to and pretend we were older than we were. I was a little more voluptuous than my sister was. So it seemed that I would get the more serious players. This was something she could not handle. So, being the oldest, she felt like she controlled me. It was like the best guy had to be hers. I never fought her, so she usually got the best guy.

Things are different now; we are both grown, and I really don't appreciate her thinking she's on top of me. So when I heard her sneaking a call to a close male friend of mine, I nearly threw her out of my house that night. She thought I was asleep, so she made a call to one of my close male friends. I heard her talking to him about what she could do to him and how she could make him hers forever. She got very graphic, and it turned my stomach. Well, that is my sister, and she is just being true to the b#@ch that she is. I really think the two of them have gotten together behind my back. I do not see that male friend very much anymore. My sister, of course, is the same as she always has been: The cat who ate the canary, just carrying on as if nothing happened.

Response:

Well it's not as if you are totally surprised, are you? You knew she was like this, but maybe you thought she had grown out of it now that she is an adult. To tell you the truth, some people never grow out of their childhood habits, and it doesn't seem like your big sister did either.

She feels she can have what she wants when it comes to you. She obviously still feels she can have the men too. If you have a serious conversation with your sister about this, maybe she will stop her actions in the future and respect you. But my advice to you is, if there is a man that you are very serious about just keep him away from your sister. It is a terrible thing to have to watch your back from your own sister. Well, all I can say is good luck to you in the future, and don't sleep on your sister.

Situation

69 After Sex He Compared Me to Other Women

R ight after we had sex, he started to compare me to other woman. It was awful; I thought he was different. I really did.

Whenever we talked, it was all about me. He never mentioned another woman ever. We have been talking to each other for more than a year, and one day we got together, and the next day he was comparing me to other woman. I told him I did not appreciate this, but he said I was being very sensitive and he was just trying to make me better. I really hated him for this. I told him I have never had a complaint about anything before.

He has the nerve to want to get together again. I don't think he appreciates me for being me, and he made me feel like I was a one-night stand or something. I have told him we cannot get together again, but he won't go away. What do you think this is?

Response:

If he is that insensitive to your feelings, maybe you don't need to deal with him anymore. If he keeps coming at you, then maybe it is just about sex. But if you are not ready to let him go, then you must realize you will have to tolerate this type of behavior from him.

This seems to be part of who he is: the sweet talker until he gets what he wants and then the real monkey-monster comes out. If this man makes you feel inferior when you have sex with him, then is it worth it? I don't think anything is worth allowing yourself to feel inferior to anyone. Maybe this lover man is just not worth it after all.

Situations 101   151

Situation

70 He Better Not Be a Down-Low

Brother

I have a male friend who is tall, dark, and absolutely handsome. He has a beautiful bald, head too. We have known
each other for two years. I have always been attracted to
him, but there have been times when I would look at him, and
he would look gay to me. Then for a while I would think he's
gay. He left town for a few months to go to work. I don't
quite know what he does. When he came back, I saw him
jogging around the park. One day I asked him if I could jog
with him, and without hesitation he said sure.

We started jogging in the mornings together and one
morning before we started to jog, he gave me one of his
business cards and he said, "I am very good too." I read the
card and it said, "Private Masseuse." I looked at him, not
knowing quite how to respond, I said, "I didn't know you
were a masseuse." He said, "Well now you know." After
thinking about it for a few days, I asked him, if he was a real
masseuse. He said, " Yes, I am a real one, this is what I do for
a living." I looked at him wondering, if I should get one or
not. He must have read my thoughts, because he said, " I have
clients, who send for me to work on them, from all over the
country."

He became my weekly masseuse and yes, girl he is great.
One day I made a pass at him and to my pleasant surprise he
took me up on it. What a great lover he is too with more than

enough equipment, if you know what I mean. We have been seeing each other once to twice a week every week.

I still can't figure out if he is completely straight or not. Although I have made love to him many times I can't be sure. It is as if there is a wall between us and I just can't get completely through to him. There is a part of him that is so guarded. With all he has going for him, he just better not turn out to be one of those down-low brothers. I am saying this because at certain times I still see some characteristics that have caused me to doubt his manhood. Now, that would be a low down dirty shame, for a man like this, to be a down-low dirty brother. Something like this could break a sisters' heart for real.

Response:

I will say I really hope you are practicing safe sex with this guy. You and he have been lovers for a while now, and you still don't really know what side of the fence he's on?

The way he gave you his card and said he was good, would make me suspicious. He may truly be a masseuse. Then again, that could be his lead in, and after a few times of massaging your body, and him giving off his subliminal messages, one's hooked, and I don't mean only on the massage, if you know what I mean.

After all of this time with him and you still can't figure him out, then maybe there is something to your question about his sexuality. If he's that good at hiding himself, then maybe there's something he is really hiding. But it is unfair for you or I to judge him at this point, because we don't have any thing solid to go on. You may have to keep digging for more clues. Good luck to finding your answers, but remember safe sex with this character is really a must. You never know if this is his M.O. It is possible that he is having sex with some if not all of his clients.

Situation

71 My Ex's Women Reveals Her Dirty Secret to Me

My ex's woman revealed her dirty secret to me. It was so unreal, like something out of a horror movie. I was invited to a holiday party; I looked around and the monster woman who broke up my relationship with my ex was standing there guzzling down drinks, and being her obnoxious self. My ex's woman was there without my ex. Believe me, my ex surely would have been embarrassed if he had seen how his woman was performing that night.

It was later that evening when she passed me in the hallway, on my way to the ladies room. When I came out of the ladies room, she said she had to talk to me. I was so tempted to ignore her and walked past her, but something told me to listen to her drunken butt. I guess it was because she was so drunk that she said the things she did. I really don't think she realized what she was doing. That's how drunk she was. I knew she was telling the truth because what she was describing about herself was definitely her character.

She started off by saying my ex is not as slick as he thinks he is. I believe he has started to cheat on her now. She went on to say that she has a very young lover in town. I said, "Oh really, and who might it be?" She laughed and said, "All I'm telling is that he is 18 years old." She told me how young he makes her feel because my ex has fallen off in certain areas of the lovemaking. I believe she started to tell me all of this because she was upset with him, and somehow she wanted to hurt him by telling me this. I guess she was getting a dose of what goes around comes round. It sounds like he is now cheating on her.

She did not stop there. The next thing she revealed was truly her dirty secret. She told me she was madly in love with this attorney. She said he is a very big attorney in another state. She told me she's with this man that she loves whenever she leaves town. She tells my ex that she's leaving town for so-called business. She laughed and said she was the slick one because my ex believes her. Then after finishing off another two drinks, she said, " But if you say anything, I will deny everything." It was getting late so I said goodnight to everyone, and I left the party. I can really destroy their relationship if I tell him, but I don't know if I should.

Response:

Wow! That truly is something. First let me say I commend you for handling her the way you did. I am sure it was not an easy thing to do, standing there listening to the monster woman. Although hearing that kind of information lets you know that all is not well in their camp.

Maybe she told you this because she was feeling kind of foolish because now she is his victim. Once you were his victim by him cheating on you with her. Now, he's cheating on her with someone else. Maybe she hates him so much that she's hoping if she told you, you would tell him.

Then again, maybe because of her guilt about doing this to you, she unconsciously was sabotaging herself. In any case, this should have made you feel pretty good in a weird way. Because now you know what they had between them is quite changed now. Regardless of why she told you, she told you. Having this information is very powerful. The best thing to do, in my opinion, is just to wait and watch the two of them crumble in their relationship. If she did want you to do her dirty work for her by telling your ex, then she would be wrong. If she just made a mistake by telling you, then let that be her burden to deal with. Now when you see your ex, your sweetest revenge on him is to smile because now you know he is being taken for a ride. He is definitely getting back what he deserves. And if you ever decide to tell him, you can do that too.

Situation

72 Don't Blame Me for What She Does

He picked an argument with me about something someone else did. A girlfriend of mine is dating my boyfriend's best friend. My boyfriend came to me and
asked me what I knew about his best friend's girl. I told him
I did not know what he was talking about. He then said, " I
bet you do." He said, " Is she fooling around on my best
friend?" I said, "I don't know."

Then my boyfriend lost his temper and started to scream
at me. My boyfriend accused me of knowing about the whole
thing. He said maybe I'm fooling around too. He started to
question me nonstop, and it went on for hours. My boyfriend
said he was so upset because his friend was hurt. I told him
not to speak to me in this manner because I had not done
anything she did.

Response:

Maybe it is time for your boyfriend to realize that he and
his best friend's relationship are two different relationships.
It was very good that you finally checked him on the way he
was speaking to you and accusing you of things when you
were innocent. It is very important that your boyfriend
understands that what is going on with his best friend has
nothing to do with you and him.

Your boyfriend needs to be mature and see that each
relationship is separate. Not only does he need to be mature;
I would suggest he needs some anger management classes. I

would hope that he handles other areas in his life better than this. This is something you need to pay close attention to. Emotional abuse of this sort can escalate into accusations that are totally unreal and worse things can happen. This could make anyone a nervous wreck.

Encourage your boyfriend to handle his temper problem. Let him know you will not tolerate this from him anymore. He will have to stop this type of treatment towards you now. If he didn't change I would be gone. Hopefully he will and the two of you will have a good and happy relationship.

Situation

73 After Summer Vacation You Treat Me Like This

How dare that S.O.B. treat me that way! Who does he think he is? So we came back to school, and a girl he was trying to talk to before school let out for summer vacation returned back to school also. So there we all are, back at school again.

Over the summer vacation this guy and I started seeing each other. He and I both live in the same city, so we became very close. It was just last week we were together and we had sex. Now that school is back and he sees this other girl again, he barely speaks to me. When he saw her, he was all over her. He even showed her more attention than he did before summer vacation.

When I saw him acting like this, I felt like cursing his ass out right there in front of her. How could he treat me this way? He should be all up under me because she is just so homely. I just don't get it, so what should I do about this?

Response:

I do understand your fury, but back up a moment, and reassess everything. Go back to the way things were just before summer vacation. Didn't you say that he was interested in her before school let out? Well, if he were interested then, why wouldn't he be interested now? I am not sure if you went after him or he came after you.

I asked you that because if he came after you, after displaying his affections for the other girl right in front of you, then he is just out for one thing, it seems. But if you went after him with thoughts to get his interest away from her, then that's another story.

Being from the same city could have made things very convenient for the two of you. Maybe you were misled by his actions. Maybe you thought by his having sex with you, he would lose all interest in the other girl. Well, as you can see, he is still interested in this other girl, and that's because, convenience or not, his desire for her has not changed.

Usually men want what they want, even if they have sex with someone else. If you went after him first, then I would say he was not interested in you, but you made yourself available and he went along with it. I can imagine you do feel awful about this; anyone would. If he continues to ignore you, then you will have to move on. You can talk to him about this, but it won't make him care about you if he really doesn't care for you like that. I'm sure he enjoyed the summer with you, but if you don't read the signs a man is showing, you can fall into traps like this over and over again. Man-stolen relationships usually don't last for long because you'll always have to be on the lookout for the next girl who will steal him from you.

Situation

74 Now That His Career is Taking Off

Now that his career is taking off, he is really showing his colors. My on-again/off-again boyfriend is listening to his older female friend; she is trying to help him in his singing career. I feel she is more than interested in his singing career.

If I mention this to my boyfriend, he snaps back and says I am jealous of her power to help him succeed in his career. This is really getting to me because I really know she digs my man. The two of them are going out of town to push his CD at a very big record company. They will be together for two weeks. I see this woman stealing my man right from under me, and I am helpless. I can't do anything about it, and he just can't see what I see.

Response:

Maybe you're right about your suspicions and maybe not. It could be that your boyfriend is really trying to make a success of himself. Maybe she is the only one that he knows who can help him to make the connections that he needs. It sounds as if you're feeling very uneasy about the whole thing because this is new to you also. But if he is going into this type of career, he will be away from you quite a bit.

What should be most important here is the trust. If he is trustworthy, I'm sure he will protect your relationship on the road, and then it does not matter what her intentions are; he will still honor you. If she is really trying to help him with no strings attached, then this could be a very good move for him to make.

Try to be strong and give a little support to him now, but you're boyfriend should show some sensitivity to your feelings now also. If in this two-week period he shows change in his feelings towards you, then become concerned and make your decisions as to what you want to do about it. I hope the two of you can work this out. If his career becomes successful, it could be an exciting, fun life together.

Situation

75 My Boyfriend Calls to Throw Me Off

M y boyfriend uses the phone to control me. He calls me all day just to hear my voice and to know what I am doing. He says when he hears my voice he can tell my frame of mind, which keeps him calm. There are times when I don't know what he is doing. It seems like he calls me first so I won't call him; I wonder if he is trying to throw me off of something.

He says he's going out with his boys sometimes, and then for hours at a time he says he's at the spa working out. During that time I cannot reach him. I am basically a homebody; I don't like to go out much.

This summer I went on vacation with my family for a week, and he stopped calling me. When I called him, he wouldn't answer his phone. I was so upset thinking about what he could be doing and why he would not answer his phone. The whole week I could not reach him. So my vacation with my family wasn't as fun as it should have been. When I got back, I asked him what happened, but he never really gave me an explanation. It was something like his phone was broken, and he tried to reach me but I must have been in an area where his phone signals could not reach.

Response:

The fact that you say he calls you all day to check on you and doesn't call you at all on your family vacation shows there is definitely something to this. It could be punishment because you went away for a week without him, especially if you don't go anywhere very much. He is not used to you not being right at home where he knows there is no chance of you maybe meeting other people.

He may be letting you know he didn't like you going away with your family for one whole week. These power-play controlling people must devastate those they want to control. If they can devastate you enough, then maybe you won't try this again. I'm sorry you did not have fun with your family because this is just what he probably wanted. Anyone who couldn't reach a boyfriend or girlfriend for a week would naturally be concerned. It seems like he wanted you to worry about what he was doing, and at the same time you will never really know if he was doing something out there or not. This is the perfect opportunity for him to accomplish two things. One-to get you back in line, and Two-to do whatever he wanted to do and at the same time blame it all on you and the decision you made to be with your family for a week. This is one time I would say look before you leap into a lifelong relationship with this guy. It's quite confining.

Situation

76 If I Am A Nut, Why Are You At My Door?

If I am a nut, then why did he want to come over to my house? This is what I asked him as he walked through my door. When it comes to this man, I act differently than I do with anybody else. I even have acted irrationally some times, and this is why I think he's pulling back. I seem to be very possessive with him, and it's because I really don't want to lose him. I really care for him.

We have been seeing each other for about three months, and I have fallen in love with him. He keeps telling me to take it slow, but his actions are showing me his deep affections towards me too. It's like he pulls me close, and then he steps back. It drives me crazy. He has told me that he loves me, and then there are nights when I can't reach him. This one time when I could not reach him, I went completely off on the phone. I accused him of being with someone else, and a lot of insecurities came out. I made several of these calls all night. When he did call me back-and that was several hours later-he told me that I was a complete nut and he was through.

After that conversation he did not call me for a week, and he would not answer my calls. Then one night he appears at my door. That's when I said to him if I am a nut, why are you at my door? He said he just wanted to see me. So he came in and we started to have sex just like that; yes, it was on. I was just so happy he was here with me. I thought I lost him forever. He never said anything about the prior week, and he didn't stay for long. I asked him to stay, but he said he had to go. I was hurt and confused, and he called me three days later just to say hey.

That was a few weeks ago, and he still remains distant. I don't quite know what he's doing. I am broken hearted, and I miss him so much. I just can't seem to pull myself together.

Response:

Three months of knowing someone is not that long. You were falling in love with him, but you were not getting to really know him. Maybe he was in a previous relationship that he was trying to get out of.

That could be a reason why you could not reach him on certain nights. He seems to be the kind of person who doesn't tell what he's doing or why. There could be many reasons why he's like this. He could even have more than one relationship going on.

It is a possibility that it could even be something you said on his phone that night that made him realize he should back up. He called you a nut; maybe he meant that he saw in you something he did not or could not deal with. But his coming to your house unannounced and having sex with you after what the two of you had been through shows he doesn't want to let you go completely.

There is one thing he seems to want to keep. Unless you want to be just his sex toy, then maybe you should look at this one a little deeper. It is obvious that you are not getting what you want from this man. Now you are getting less of him than you had before. I don't think a situation like this gets better. I'm not saying to let him go because it is obvious to me you are not strong enough to at this point. But you better start to get a grip on yourself, and look for other people in your life. It's really not good when a woman is this much into a man and he is not feeling her the same way. Get it together, girl.

Situation

77 I Love You Deeply but Hate You More

I t is so difficult for me to come to grips with the fact that the one I love so deeply doesn't understand how to love me back. This gives me no option but to let our relationship go. This makes me realize that you can hate a person you love as much as you love him.

Although the thought of not being with him is very painful and it's like waking up to that black cloud every day, I really have to get out of this dead-end relationship because I know it's going nowhere. But every time I think about letting go, I just can't. I feel sick just thinking about leaving him. It's like it's better to have this bad relationship and be with him than not to have him at all.

We've been together six years now, so it's not that easy to just let go. Each year things get worse for us. I don't think he wants this relationship like I do. I know I have to do something, but it is so hard to end this relationship because I love him, and I always wanted so much for it to be the two of us. That's why I love him but hate him more. Because it's all on him, it's his decision. I can do nothing but wait for him. That's if he decides to let our relationship work.

Response:

I understand that this can be a very painful reality to face. But this is your life too, and you will have to take a more responsible attitude about things. To love someone this deeply and the reciprocation is just not there or not on the same level, then you're right-a choice must be made. But I think it is your choice to make now.

It seems as if he has made his choice, but you don't want to see it. To stay in a relationship like this would mean for you to lose your dignity. I say this because it's as if you are begging for him to stay with you. It would be like having part of him and not having all of you all at the same time. It would be like compromising yourself to be with someone who will not give you all of him. It would be this way because he is not interested in you the way you are in him. In a relationship like this, much of what you need and want will continue to be ignored.

I know you keep saying why can't he just love me right, but it's not this way with the two of you. For whatever reason, the two of you are not feeling the same way about each other. When there is always conflict either within the relationship or within oneself about the relationship, then the two of you will have no peace together. That's why you feel love and hate at the same time. You are frustrated with the relationship.

Sometimes love is like this and if so, you'll have to realize that the relationship is just not working. Maybe you can suggest some sort of counseling, but this must be something the two of you decide you want to do together for your relationship. I would say if you can't, save this relationship, then save your dignity and get out.

Situation

78 My Ex Saw Me in My New Man's Hummer

I t was sweet revenge stepping out of my new man's, Hummerâ. Yes, sweet revenge came when I least expected it. My new boyfriend and I were in the mall parking lot, and while I was getting out of my new boyfriend's brand new Hummerâ, I saw my ex-boyfriend a few cars over.

Yes, he was still driving his four year-old Explorer truck. My ex just stared at me as if shocked to see me. The last time I saw him was six months ago at his house. He told me it was over between us, and I was the shocked one then. He walked away from me that day and left me standing there, crying.

My new boyfriend is absolutely gorgeous; he is 6 ft. 2 in. and has a great body. In fact he has just been drafted into the NFL. I could see my ex was very upset; he tried to keep his composure, but I know him and he was upset. He must remember that he broke up with me and could care less. My new man and I headed into the mall. Oh, yes, this was truly sweet revenge, and I loved every second of it. Now my ex is calling me and just blowing up my phone, leaving messages like he still loves me and he would like to see me again. He says he's with no one and he misses me. Oh, really!

Response:

Well, that is sweet revenge. The fact that he broke up with you and left you standing there, crying, makes seeing him now even sweeter. Now that he has seen you with someone new, he wants to profess his love to you. Maybe now he's starting to realize he lost a good woman. Maybe now he is also starting to realize he can't find a woman that is right for him. There are a lot of "maybes" here, and maybe after seeing you with someone else and you seem happy, it made him jealous.

I say beware of your ex because he could be trying to stop what you have with your new man, or he could be trying to tap into old feelings you had for him. He could be trying to pull you back into him emotionally to show himself that he is still the one. Or he could be trying to show your new man that he is still strong in your heart.

You should not trust his intentions at this point. You should not let him destroy or even think he can destroy what you are trying to build with your new man. I don't see why you would, but if you do respond to his calls, proceed with caution.

Situation

79 My Step Sister is Now With My Ex

That's right: my stepsister was caught with my ex. One night I decided to go to this club that a friend of mine was opening up. I went alone to the club because I was going to meet him there. I was sitting there waiting for him when I realized my stepsister and four of her girlfriends were there also. I walked over to her and was happy to see her. I had not seen her in a long while. She told me she came with some friends that we both knew.

Then I saw my ex sitting at her table with her other friends. I then said, "Is that my ex?" She said, "Yes it is." She never gave me another word of explanation. I looked at her, and believe me I was shocked. I remained calm and walked over to where he was sitting.

He smiled and said hello, and the look I gave him told him how I felt. It was a look that said, "You dirty, nasty thing, you!" I looked at the both of them, and shook my head and went to another section of the club to wait for my friend. I am still boiling mad about this, but I have not said or done anything yet because I don't want to do or say the wrong thing to these two fools.

What puzzles me is that my ex and I were still cool after we broke up. So why didn't he respect me enough to not let this happen or to at least tell me they were now friends? Girl, as my friend, can you tell me how I should handle this? P-l-e-a-s-e.

Response:

Your stepsister obviously has no respect for you or herself if she would do something like this. You're right not to do anything until you are sure what you should do. Sometimes the best thing to do is nothing at all until you have talked to your ex and asked the questions that are on your mind.

In any case, whether you talk to them or not, they are still dating or, at least, friends. If you no longer have feelings for your ex, then let him go. The fact that you know he is a conniving, deceptive person that you are no longer with should be good enough. It is sure better to know this about him than not to know. Now that you do know, you can scratch him off of your " We're Still Cool List." As far as your stepsister is concerned, there could be so many unre-solved issues here. How close were the two of you growing up? Was there competition between the two of you? One thing you have learned is not to trust her around any of your future boyfriends. She is not a very good stepsister to you. I always say it's better to know than not know.

Situation

80 My 4 Men Equals One Man

I come up with one whole man after I put all four of these men together. I know this sounds ridiculous, but this is actually how it is. I would love to have just one man, but it is hard to find one man with even half the qualities or values I am looking for. I have even lowered my standards considerably in order to find that one man.

I feel I am forced into a lifestyle I never wanted. I don't want to be with four men at the same time. First of all, it's a lot of work. And if I don't want to do anything else in my life, than dealing with four men at the same time could exhaustingly be done. Having four frogs is not my idea of a Prince Charming. I'm kidding; all of these guys are really nice guys. But I feel cheated as a woman if I date only one of them.

These are the reasons why I date them. I date # 1 man because sexually he and I are very compatible. We have a great sex life, but once out of bed, nothing else works in our relationship. I date # 2 man because he is very caring and generous with everything. He takes me to very nice places for dinner and he buys me beautiful presents. He is a total gentleman to me. He doesn't have a lot of time to spend with me because he works very hard and is always out of town. I only see him once or twice a month.

I date #3 man because he is very creative and fun to be around. We go out to clubs, bars, concerts, and if I need to talk to someone or just need a friend, he is always there for me. Our relationship is mostly platonic but we have sex sometimes. I date#4 man because he is the man I truly love. I love him from the bottom of my heart. I have been dating him for five years now. But I know our relationship will not go any further because of his other responsibilities, and he has always been honest and up front with me right from the start.

He is not married, and he is not living with anyone. That's why I stay in this relationship with him. Maybe I'm still hoping it will be the two of us one day. I am tired of this lifestyle and I really do want one man, but I can't find the right one. Help! I want a simple life with one man that is right for ME.

Response:

Wow! You are a busy girl; do you have any time for yourself, ever? It seems to me that maybe you should look at the fourth man first. This seems to be the longest and strongest of all your relationships. Have you ever thought that maybe this fourth relationship is the culprit? I say the culprit because it seems as though you have surrounded yourself with these other men because this fourth man's relationship with you is so stagnant. This man has told you he was not going to marry you or be with you. Nevertheless, you are still holding on to the one-of-these days fairy tale with him. I do believe you are stuck in this relationship, and it's not allowing you to experience a full relationship with another man.

I really believe when you are ready to face the truth about these relationships, you will find your man. Once you close the door on a go-no-where relationship, then the right man for you will walk through that door. Yes, I am sure there is a man out there waiting just for you, but you'll have to be ready for him. Set your priorities straight, and I'm sure you can have what: you really want: one man that is right for you. You may not want to hear this, but I am sure your love or life ever after is not with man #4. The only way this relationship will ever work would be for you and him to get real about your relationship. If you love him, then he should be enough just the way he is. If not; then move on and find your "One" man. The one and only, the love of your life, the real love ever after, the prince charming you are looking for; I really don't know if all of this really exist in one man, but I do know there is one man out there for you. You just have to be ready for him when he comes.

Situation

81 He Is Everything I Never Wanted

ooks can be deceiving. I met this man, who is really not my type. I met him at my night class at the University. He is a very calm, easy, and peaceful person. One day he asked me about my class, and that's how we got into a conversation. One evening he asked if I would go have coffee with him after class, and I said yes. When I say he is not my type, he isn't. I really shouldn't be so shallow, but he is not handsome although he does have something.

He wears these funny-looking dreads but they are neat and they have the greatest smell. The smell actually caught my attention. It was like a perfume, oil. He told me he had it specially made for his hair. He is about 20 or 30 lbs. heavier than I like my men. His clothes are really very stylish, and he looks great in them. He invited me to his house in a very affluent neighborhood. When I walked into his beautifully decorated home, he was in the kitchen cooking, the table was set with wine and roses, and I was totally impressed.

Everything was great-the music, the fireplace, everything. Once I walked into his beautiful bedroom, I did not want to leave. His bed was beautiful and inviting, and he had great mirrors on the ceiling. He gave me the body massage after he undressed me. We made love. I have never felt this special before. He made me feel so loved, admired, and appreciated. What I noticed was that his skin was like satin. I have never felt skin as soft and as smooth as his.

Everything about this man was a wonderful surprise to me. We have been dating for six months now, and he is truly as wonderful as he seems. He may not be physically beauti- ful, but everything about him is. Because of his ways with me, I now see him as beautiful. I truly have fallen in love with this man. My girlfriends are shocked that I have fallen for him. They can't believe it.

Response:

Well, I know you said he is everything you never wanted, but it looks like he is everything you ever wanted. This is truly a case of "looks are deceiving." You did say he had something about him.

I am glad for you, that you didn't let being shallow stop what turned out to be a good thing for you. Your friends would only wish they could be so lucky. You did learn something from that night class: Don't judge a book by its cover just read it. All I can say is good luck to you and your man.

Situation

82 Internet Love, So He Says

This guy advertised on a singles love site on the Internet. He said he wanted desperately to find love because he is recently out of a relationship. He physically described what type of woman he liked, but also added that the woman should be well off and independent. The woman he described was definitely, me. He even said if she has kids that would be fine. I knew this was me, because I have kids too.

I answered his ad, and we met for the first-time in a public place. He chose a very beautiful upscale restaurant, and he paid for everything with his gold MasterCard. When he drove up, I remember saying to myself, " What a beautiful car he has." The way this man was dressed it seemed like he stepped out of GQ magazine. He was definitely everything he described. And I definitely like it.

Everything was going well for a few weeks; then he disappeared for a month. When he did call me again, he said he had to leave town because his mother was ill. I believed him and by this time really wanted to go to bed with him. So I did; he then asked me if I would invest in a big venture he was involved in. I invested thousands, and when I was supposed to get my return, he told me the deal fell through. I was quite upset with him, but what could I do?

One day I went to his house unexpected, and I saw this woman coming out of his house. What got me was that she looked like a clone of me. I waited until she got in her car and drove away, and I followed her. I honked my horn for her to stop, and she did.

I introduced myself, and we continued to talk. I found out he met her the same way he met me, and she gave up money too. I have realized this man was some kind of pampered pimp. And we were the women he was pimping. I am not sure how to approach him. If I let him know I'm on to him, I may never get my money back.

Response:

If you don't let him know you're on to him you may never get your money back either. From what you have described about him, it seems as though you like him very much. Are you sure you are not using the money thing so that you can stay involved with him? If you are sure this is what he is doing, then why don't you get away from him and bring him to court to get your money? When you meet characters like this on the Internet, they can be anything they say they are. You really don't know this man and what his background is. He could be involved with a lot of things. In a case like this, your best bet is to move on.

You can try to sue him for your money or say it's a bad investment and leave it at that. If I were you, I would be more careful about Internet dating. These types of relationships can be very scary. Maybe he does this all the time, and how would you know? This time you lost money, but the next time you could lose more than money. My advice to you is to find out a lot more about these people before you trust them with your money or your life. Be Cautious; be Safe. Remember, a pimp can come in all different shapes, colors, or sizes. It's not what a man looks like that makes him a pimp; it's the fact that a man will take money from a woman that makes him a pimp.

Situation

83 My New Friend Is My Man's Ex-Woman

I met a very nice woman at the nail salon. She and I were just talking about stuff in general, and we just clicked. I wanted to make friends with her because I really admired her. She is beautiful, smart, and totally together. She said she likes to go out, and she said maybe she and I could go out together sometime. She told me she broke up with her man a few months ago, and she was ready to start dating again. I told her, "Let's exchange numbers." Since my nails were wet, I told her to give me her number, and I would call her to give her mine.

Upon leaving the nail shop, I must have dropped her number somewhere. I had lost her number, so I went back to the nail shop to give my number to the woman who did our nails, in case she came in again. But she never called. So, months later, my man described this woman and said her name and he asked me if I knew her. I asked him why, and he said because since my name is so unique and not many people have it, when he said my name and described me to this person, she said she met me in the nail shop. I was so happy he found her.

I asked my boyfriend if he had her number, I told him that I had been looking for her. My boyfriend said in a strange tone that he bumped into her today and she asked him who, he was dating these days, and he said my name. My boyfriend said, "Baby, you can't be friends with her; she is my ex girlfriend." I was shocked and disappointed and upset all at the same time. I don't know if I should be upset or jealous or what because this woman is all of that. What if he bumps into her again? This feels weird.

Response:

I can imagine it does feel strange. It's not like the two of you were real friends. What she and your boyfriend had was before you, so that should not have any effect on you and your man now. Well, look at it in a positive way. Your boyfriend came right out and told you about her. He told you he used to date her, and he told you he saw her. If he was still interested in her, he might not have told you anything.

She seems like maybe she would have been a good friend for you, but I'm sure you will find another friend. At least you can see why your boyfriend dated her. I guess that's why he is dating you now. He has good taste. It's not a bad thing. Let it go, and enjoy your relationship with your new boyfriend. He's yours now, not hers.

Situation

84 He Had The Nerve To Wear A Magnum Condom

I could not believe what I was looking at. We were about to have sex, so he put his condom on. All is well and good, right? Wrong! His condom was a magnum condom, so when I looked at it he only fit into it halfway, so you can imagine what that looked like, having all that rubber left on top just hanging there. That's right; the rest of the condom was just there unused.

It was totally disgusting to me, and I could not believe he thought everything was just fine. I just didn't have the guts to tell him differently. Do you think he really thought he should wear a very big condom on an average-size penis? He seemed so comfortable with wearing it too. It was just such a turnoff that I couldn't wait until this episode was over. He is truly a great guy and his conversations are terrific, but this big condom thing is just too weird for me. Is he for real or what? Is he a little off or what?

Response:

I guess that could be a very strange thing to see and probably stranger to feel. If this guy doesn't know better, then maybe you should find out more about his sex life. If you're interested in him, then maybe you should find out what type of women he deals with.

It is possible that he may deal with very inexperienced females who just don't know any different. I do feel if he deals with experienced women, someone should have surely alerted him to this at some point. Or maybe the ones that knew better felt the same way you did. They may not have wanted to hurt his feelings because he is such a great guy in many other ways. It would be interesting to find out if he ever had a long relationship with anyone. Hey, maybe he was hoping you didn't noticed, Hah Hah!!! I can't imagine what was up with that. Maybe the next time you should buy the condoms if there is a next time.

Situation

85 He Wants To Move In Already

He asked me if he could move in with me. I knew it was coming, we've only known each other for one month, and I knew it was coming. We met at a club, and he is really fine. Almost before he asked me my name he asked me where I live.

He questioned if I live alone or with someone. Then he asked me what I do for a living. I guess he was auditioning his next victim, little ole me. I say "victim" because that is exactly what I felt like. I felt like I was his prey, and he was my predator.

He doesn't work and has no place to live. At the moment he is at his mother's place. He says he just got in from out of town. He said he just gave up his place and is trying to start over here. Even though he has no place of his own to live and he doesn't have a job yet, he does have the latest cell phone.

After our rather long conversation I've come to realize that "just moving back in town" means no more than he's been living right here in town. So he's been back-and-forth to his mom's house for the past two years. He's been living right here in town. I thought he had a big business deal going the way he stayed on his cell phone the whole time he is trying to hold a conversation with me. I guess that's why our conversation was rather long because half of that time he was on his cell phone talking to some other people. I kept wondering to myself, "Who's paying that large phone bill of his? It's not him, I'm sure." He has no job, remember.

After that evening, we began to talk frequently and a few weeks later I let him come over and he stayed that evening and the next evening. I then realized he wasn't about to leave. I told him I had to go out of town, so he would have to leave. He did, but the very next weekend when he came over again he popped the question. The question was, could he move in with me. I guess our short-lived romance is over now because I told him," Hell no, you cannot move into my place." Would you believe he was upset with me? I guess he figured he invested a whole month on me and didn't get what he wanted, a place to stay. Oh, yes, the predator broke up with me. I guess he's moving on to his next victim. I guess he said, "Why waste any more time with this one." I am totally O.K. with that, as long as I am the prey who got away.

Response:

I am glad to see you handled this matter in the way that you did. You saw it coming, and you were prepared for it. Even though he was so called "fine," you did not let that cloud your rational thinking. You looked out for yourself. I guess you know now who was paying for his phone. If it was not his mother then it probably was some other victim, just as long as it was not you. Great Escape, Girl!

Situation

86 I'm Not Sure Who The Father Is

I made a very big mistake of having unprotected sex with two men in the same month. I now don't know which one fathered my child. I am trying to figure this mess out; I am totally upset with myself right now. See, I was breaking up with one guy whom I truly love and rebounding with the other guy whom I don't love.

I have never had unprotected sex with more than one man within the same month before because I never wanted to be in the predicament that I am in right now. I just didn't follow my own rule this time. I'm pregnant, and I don't know which man fathered my baby.

This is truly a nightmare because if the baby is for the man that I truly love, I really want this baby. But if it's for the rebounder, then I definitely do not want it. I don't know what to do now.

Response:

Yes, you are right: this is a very difficult situation for you. There is not much advice I really could give you because you already know you let things get out of hand. I say "out of hand" because having unprotected sex with both men in the same month, and you get pregnant, you know there is no way for you to be sure which one is the father.

I hate to imagine the dilemma you are in wanting the baby if it's for the man you love and definitely not wanting it if it's for the other man. I can imagine you are an emotional wreck.

Because it is your body, any decision is a personal one, and you will have to make that decision on your own. I just hope you find the right answers within yourself so that you can make the right choices for yourself. Whatever decisions you make, let this circumstance be a big lesson to you, one you will never have to repeat again.

Situation

87 I Asked Him for Money Before We Had Sex

When I asked him for some money to pay my rent, I told him I would pay him back, but that was before we had sex. Our relationship before we had sex was strictly, business. I am thinking that after I asked him for the money, he felt more comfortable in pursuing me sexually.

I am not sure if that is it, but recently we moved into another direction with our relationship. We have had sex a few times since then, and he did give me the money just like he said he would, but now I feel I should not pay him back the money. But because I said I would, I feel I should, and because we had sex I feel I shouldn't.

Response:

Well you said you would pay him back the money, and as a business deal you should. Now that the relationship has changed into something sexual, I can understand your point.

Maybe at this point in the relationship with him the two of you can discuss this. I would say discuss it because you told him you would pay it back. Maybe he will agree with you, and insist you just keep the money. If he does, and you still feel strongly about repaying him, then maybe you can buy him a very nice present instead. I'm sure if he's a gentleman the two of you can certainly work this out one way or another.

Situation

88 He Just Sits Around Wearing Click Clacks

My man is attentive and sensitive to my feelings, but I get so sick and tired of seeing him sitting around the house all day every day with no job and wearing these click clacks in his hair. He thinks he's Snoop Dog or some other rapper. I get out and go to work every day. Ever since I met him, he has been talking about this lawsuit that's going to come through for him, and that was six months ago and nothing has come through yet.

I came home one day, much earlier than I usually do. There was this girl sitting in the living room, combing his hair into two ponytails and putting these big-ass click clacks around them. I was furious, and he just sat there as if it was no big deal. He said she was just a friend. I believe there is something more to it. I also believe she comes over a lot when I am at work. He just got caught this time, that's all. I am not sure if this relationship between him and me is really going anywhere. I just hope he is not using me.

Response:

Maybe you're right: this could be something he has done before when you were at work. But as far as work is concerned, I'm not sure whether he'll get a job or not. Maybe this is the way he lives. Was he working before six months ago? This is the question you need to ask him. If he was working before six months ago or before the accident, then it is possible that he will get a job again. But if he was not working or has never had a job, then maybe he will not be getting a job any time soon.

There seems to be a lot of stuff going on here. Let's look at the positive in this relationship. You said that he is attentive and sensitive to your feelings; then he might be receptive to your concerns if you sit down and explain them to him. Maybe then he will explain to you why he is not motivated enough to go to work. One thing you should do is let him know your feelings about having a female in the house when you're not at home. Whether this relationship works out or not is up to the two of you and what you will accept or not accept.

Situation

89 He Is Sooo Scornful

He is a very scornful man. If something goes wrong in our relationship or if I do something he feels is an injustice to him even if it isn't, he's out for war. If I make a decision that he does not like or if I say my opinion and it's not in line with his, retaliation will soon come and always when I least expected it.

It is not a physical war, but an emotional one. I am becoming a nervous wreck in this relationship. We have been together for three years. Everything we have we've gotten together. Recently I was laid off of my job, so I depend on him right now. But this is the thing he did that is making me question whether I want to stay with him or not.

It was basically a simple thing, but it was cruel to me. He promised me he would buy me my favorite perfume for my birthday. When my birthday came, there was no perfume. When I asked why, he said it was because I was late picking him up from work three times last month. That was the straw that broke the camels back for me. I'm really thinking about leaving him. I just can't take this much longer.

Response:

This seems as if you're in a relationship where there's no-win for you. It seems as if it's his-way-or you'll-pay type of relationship. He seems as if he is into the power or control thing. His behavior toward you in this relationship is abusive.

He sabotages your confidence and judgment. If people are afraid to make decisions or to say their opinion because they're afraid of the consequences thereafter, then they are in an abusive relationship.

These relationships make them feel less than who they are. I really hope you look at this relationship for what it is so that you can find a more supportive and healthy one. Maybe you might want to be alone for a while. Whatever you decide to do, you need peace and comfort instead of fear and shock. And on a girl's birthday is not the time to try and teach a lesson like he did.

Situation

90 She Changed His Old House to New

I have not seen my boyfriend in three months. So I decided to visit him after his repeated phone calls asking me to come over. I go over there to his house, and his house has completely changed. It is so well organized and there are long stemmed flowers in glass vases, even the fish tank he always talked about he got with beautiful exotic fish in it.

I was really impressed until I saw a picture of a woman on his mantle. I didn't ask him who she was because I felt that was what he wanted me to do. So I acted as if I never saw it. I don't know what to think about this. Do you think there is another woman in his life now?

Response:

I am not sure if there is another woman in his life or not, but at this point there could be. Maybe he is trying to show you he has moved on but still wants you, or maybe he's trying hard to make you jealous. If he is trying to make you jealous, maybe it's because he's hoping you and he will get back together. Sometimes men do strange things to spark a woman's interest, and maybe this is one of them.

The picture of the woman could be part of his trying to get you jealous. If it is, it's there to make you come back faster. If you care for him, it would be the time now to show it.

Situation

91 He's Never Available When I Call

I believe my live-in boyfriend is having an affair at his office. He's never available when I call him at the office. We just had a baby together, so I am a stay-at-home mom. He is an advertising consultant and works closely with graphic art designers.

There is this one woman he has been working closely with for a few months now. I believe he is having an affair with her. He has told me that he has ADD – Attention Deficit Disorder and that his attention span is short which causes him to get bored very quickly. He did tell me he had this disorder when we first got together, but he didn't act strange or anything, so I thought he was fine. He has had one other affair earlier in our relationship. He blamed his action on his disease. He said the affair meant nothing.

He has gotten help for this disorder or at least he told me he did. He tells me all the time that he loves me, and I want to believe him. It is always in the back of my mind that this affair problem we have will keep happening throughout our relationship. I'm just not sure how to handle this.

Response:

Since you knew of this disorder early in the relationship, why didn't you find out more about it then? You should have found out what this disorder is all about before bringing a child into the relationship. This way you would know what is involved with dealing with a person who has ADD.

It may be the disorder that is causing this behavior or it could be him using this disorder as an excuse to behave this way. You need to find out more about ADD.

He said he loves you and if you love him, this is the only way to start to find out what part is the disease and what part is your boyfriend wanting to do these things on his own. Consider really finding out more about the ADD disorder because you and he have a child to raise. This could answer if your child will have this disorder also. This should give you clarity about where you stand in his life. I am sure this will give you peace of mind also.

Situation

92 Playboy Got Kicked to the Curb

I t was a weird week with my new boyfriend and me. Things started to get a little strange on Friday. He met me after work, and we were supposed to go to dinner. I was excited to see him. As soon as I got in the car, he said he had to go to rehearse tonight. He plays the saxophone for a band. He said he could not take me to dinner. Instead of going to dinner here I am being dropped off at my front door. It went from bad to worse. A few hours later I called him. I got no answer. My new boyfriend did not call me until Saturday the next day at 3:00 p.m.

When he called me he told me that rehearsal went on very late and he did not want to disturb my sleep in the middle of the night. He asked me what I was doing, and I told him I was doing my hair. He said when I finished would I call him back. I said I would, and I did two hours later. There was no answer all night. The next day, Sunday, we were supposed to go to the evening service at church. He called me at 4:00 p.m. to see if I was going. I told him I was not going; he said fine. I got dressed and I went anyway. I got there early and sat in my car. My new boyfriend drove up with one of the women from the church. I didn't even go in to service that evening. I left and went home.

He called me up after service, but I didn't answer. The message he left me was that he was going to stay around the church real late and he would talk to me tomorrow, Monday. When I didn't get a call all day Monday, I went around to his house. The light was on but he was not at home. I sat there, and at 2 o'clock in the morning I left. Because he was still not home. It is now Friday night and no call since. This is the man who said we should hold back on sex until we get to know each other better. But we are not to have sex with anybody else either. This was his idea; yeah right!

Response:

Your new boyfriend seems like a real character. It seems as if he is quite busy. He also seems as if he knows how to bend the truth. That's a deceptive person. It doesn't seem as if he's being truthful with you. The early stages of a new relationship should not start with all of this ducking and darting going on.

It's a good thing he said to wait on sex until the two of you get to know each other better. This way you can wait and see if he is worth it or not. Even though he doesn't want you to have sex with anyone, it doesn't seem like that rule applies to him. I think you know what you have here. There are some people who hide behind the church thing. They act like they are so holy and therefore you may not question their motives. But these types are the worse. One should never hide behind the church to do their dirt. I really think your little playboy needs to get kicked to the curb. Don't waste another minute playing the peek-a-boo game with him. If he doesn't want to be where you are, then be where he'll never be and that is around you. Don't wait on this one.

Situation

93 He Found Out My Real Age

I didn't tell him my age because he is so much younger than I am. Besides, when he guessed my age it was so much younger than I really am. He guessed my age to be 28 years old. He is 24, and I am 35 years old. He and I were having a great time together for three months. We went to a club one night, and the woman at the door asked for my I.D. I really was very flattered. I gave her my driver's license and she said very loudly that she could not believe I was born in the year I was born. Yes, she said my year out loud.

That was the first time my new man knew my real age. He was shocked, and I could tell things were immediately different. I was furious at that B#t$h. Until then he and I had the greatest times. He would call me and take me to dinner almost every night, we went to concerts, he would ride me on his Harley Davidson bike, and we were just great together. This happened about two weeks ago, and just last week he called me and asked why I didn't tell him my real age. He must be really upset because he hasn't called me since then.

Response:

Maybe he was really into you and he was OK with the four-year difference until he found out it was an 11 year difference. Maybe that was too much for him to handle. This is sometimes the risk you take for not being honest about your age; sometimes people leave. Sometimes it's the way they find out that makes the difference.

Some men are fine with the age difference thing, and some are just not OK with it at all. The comforting thing is; it seems as if he really liked you for you, no matter what your age. It is really sad now that he knows your age it has made a difference in his feelings toward you. I understand this can really bother a person if he or she is hung up on the age thing. But age is truly a number, and to let go of a good relationship because of age is truly his loss.

If age bothers him that much, then maybe it is better for you that he found out sooner than later. Investing more time in a person that feels this way about age would have been more than a waste of time for you, and I am sure you would have been hurt a lot deeper. Try and remember from now on that it is better to be upfront about your real age, and just be grateful that you look so good that you are taken for younger.

But don't make this age thing your problem; you are your age, and there is nothing you can do to change that, but it seems as if your boyfriend has the problem with age, and this is something he'll have to deal with. I hope he gets over it and the two of you continue with your great relationship. If not, you are a great person, and I'm sure you will have no problems meeting someone who will care for you just the way you are at this age or any age to come.

Situation

94 I Hate This Dumb B#$#ard

He left me after he was very irresponsible with me. That's right; he broke up with me right after I had unprotected sex with him. This was the first time that I did not use a condom with him. I felt that we were drifting apart, and this was something he always wanted-sex with me without a condom. I gave in to him in my desperate attempt to bring him close to me again.

I really do love this man with all of my heart, and I never want to lose him. But the very next day, he called me and told me he wanted to break up with me. I was shocked and devastated, and all I kept thinking was that I hate this dumb b#$#ard. For two months I felt like I was living a nightmare. I thought I was pregnant; my period did not come. I went to the doctor, he took tests, and he told me I was not pregnant but under severe stress. My period stopped because I was under stress from my ex-boyfriend.

I was totally relieved that I was not pregnant. When I got back home, I called my ex and told him that I was waiting for the pregnancy results. A few days later, my period came. The shock of that b#$#ard breaking up with me like that stopped my period.

He has been calling me and saying he is going crazy not knowing if I'm pregnant or not. I should let him worry indefinitely or at least nine months. I don't know if that's what I should do, but I hate him that much that it would be easy for me to deceive him like that by not telling him that I am not pregnant but under stress.

Response:

The fact that you are telling me about it lets me know that you don't think you should deceive him this way. I realize this was a severe blow and shock to you at the time. There was a lot to deal with at one time, such as having sex with him without a condom, which was not something you wanted to do, but you did that for him but against your better judgment: then the pressure of not knowing if you had gotten pregnant. I believe anyone would go into shock and devastation from something like this, especially if you did not see it coming.

You should never lose yourself to anyone like this. Relationships break up; it is not the end of the world. Now that you know you are not pregnant, it may be better for you to tell him you are not pregnant. Now that you see the type of man he is – selfish, irresponsible and especially not sensitive to you or your needs – you must know you are better off without him.

If you don't see it yet, I'm sure you will. I know you may want him to suffer the way you did for two months. But I am sure he won't get away with treating people this way for very long. He will meet his match. Remember, "Revenge is mine says the Lord." Don't be vengeful; just get over him, the sooner the better. Try to move on from here, and let this self-centered jerk go. Also there is a lesson in every experience; I hope you have learned your lesson in this one.

Situation

95 My Ex-Man Called Me Crying

y ex husband called me crying-not just a sniffle or two but breathtaking, agonizing, gut-wrenching crying. That's right-big old crocodile tears. I let him cry a few minutes before I asked him what was wrong. He said he didn't know what to do. Even though he is my ex, we have remained friends. He and I divorced five years ago, but we had been married for seven years before that. He got remarried again two years ago.

So in between his crying those crocodile tears, I asked him where his wife was, and in between more tears I heard him say she moved out six months ago. I didn't want to say "I told you so," so I didn't. But I told him so. I knew she was not right for him; she is 26 years old, he is 37 years old, and I am 31 years old. Do you know this idiot couldn't wait to tell me he was marrying a woman who is younger than me! Knowing him like I do, I knew it would not work because it seemed that besides the age, she was not his type at all. She left him after a year to be with her ex-boyfriend who is much younger than my ex husband. Her ex (the man she ran back to) is 26 or 27 also. See, her ex boyfriend was her high school sweetheart. I heard that they never got over each other. This is information that I never told my ex because he couldn't handle it.

My ex asked me if he should file for a divorce from his new wife since it has been six months and she refuses to come back home. I asked him if he still loved her, and he said yes. I then told him if he still loved her, then he is not ready to file for a divorce.

I also told him to stick it out and hold on to her. I said, "Why let her go if you are not ready to let her go?" He said O.K. and thanked me for the advice. I wonder if I should have stayed out of it altogether and let him figure this mess out his damn self?

Response:

It seems as if there still are some unresolved issues between the two of you. But as for the advice you gave your ex, I would say that it was good advice. If that is exactly how you feel about the situation, then the advice was fine. But if you told him to stay in the relationship because you thought it would cause him more pain, then that is not the best advice you could have given him.

If you truly have his best interest at heart, then I believe the advice you gave him was correct. Why make a move such as divorce proceedings if this is not what is in the heart to do. You were just being a good friend. It is obvious that he is not ready to see the truth about this woman. I don't think she loves him the way she loves her ex boyfriend. It is obvious your ex does not want to see the truth about this relationship.

Situation

96 Found Love on Our Children's Class Field Trip

My girlfriend, this man and I both have children in the same class. There was a class field trip a few months ago and that's where it started. Some parents go on the class trips to help the teacher out with the kids. My girlfriend and I mentioned how handsome this guy was, and now he was on the field trip with us.

In order to save gas, we all went in my girlfriend's new car. The kids went on the school bus. So the three of us met the teacher and the kids at the science fair. It was after spending a few hours together on the field trip that Mr. Handsome came right out and said he would like to take me out sometime. I was excited, and I said sure. We exchanged numbers and my girlfriend said, "Go for it and when you're through with him let me have him." We laughed and that was that.

Since then, he and I have been seeing each other. Since he works at home and his wife goes to work every day and I am a stay-at-home mom and my husband goes to work every day, everything is so perfect. We see each other almost every day. I am in total love with him, but we are married with kids in the same class. I don't know what to do. It was supposed to be just a fling and that was all. Now I am more worried about what he's doing whenever he's not around me than I am worried about my own husband.

Response:

It does seem like you're in a little too deep. This was not supposed to happen in the first place. I guess you have to watch what you wish for because you may get it. I guess you got it. It seems like a big headache to me. My only suggestion to you would be to really look at this for real and not like two grown kids on a school field trip. It may be fun to flirt a little here and there, but know when to stop it.

These types of things are always dangerous and risky. The ones to think about here are your kids. Your responsibility is to keep them protected and cared for. Remember, you are their parents; if you don't look out for them, then no one will. If this gets to them and then your mates find out, it will no doubt destroy both your families I'm sure. This is your family and your life and your decision to make. If this man's thing with you is more important than your children's security and well being, then just think about how worried you are about what he is doing when you are not around him. What if he starts to see someone else; you can't control that. Then what about the fact that you may mess up your family and children and you still don't have this man? My advice to you is let this web of deception go. I don't care how good it is to you now; there is no guarantee with this man. Don't be selfish. Think of your beautiful happy children first because they depend on you for everything, so don't let them down. If you wanted another answer, then I'm not the one to ask.

Situation

97 No He Didn't Throw Me Out

M y boyfriend and I were sitting in front of his fireplace. We were talking, and everything was fine. We were getting cozy, and I asked him to give me back my diary that he claimed I left over his house. I believe he was snooping in my stuff when he came over to my house. I believe he found my diary in my drawer and just kept it.

First of all, my diary has been missing for three months now. I was losing my mind trying to find it; then one day I asked my boyfriend if he had seen it or if I had left it over his house. I know I did not leave it at his house because I never take it out of my house. I said this in case he did take it, so he can give it back because he can say I left it there; that way I won't accuse him of stealing it. He then came out and said yes, he did see it. He said he saw it on his bed one day and he put it away for me.

I felt violated because now I knew he had read all of my private thoughts and that was the reason he had been treating me differently; he had changed towards me. He was not treating me the same. I told him I wanted him to give me back my diary now. He kept saying that he would, but he couldn't find it right now. I had a feeling he never intended to give me back my diary. He said he wanted to have sex first; then I said, "No, I want my book first." We got into an argument, and out of the clear blue sky, he became strange. I had never seen him like this before I was truly frightened; he looked like he transformed into the incredible Hulk or something.

He told me to get out of his house right now before he did something he would regret. He ran me out of his house, he was screaming, "Get out of my house, right now!" I left, and on my way home he called me saying he couldn't find the damn book now, but he would look for it. I didn't answer, so he left the message on the service. I never want to talk to him or see him again, but I want my diary back.

Response:

I don't know what was in your diary, but your boyfriend seems to have been affected by it. If he was snooping around and found it and stole it, then he was wrong. It is a violation of your privacy, and I do understand how you feel. The first thing to be concerned about is his violence toward you. If you have never seen this in him before, then it's a good thing that you did. Now you know what kind of person you're dealing with.

When a person is upset or deeply hurt, he or she may act many different ways. He may just be reacting to what he read in your diary. What you should have done was make sure that your diary was in a very secure place in your home. When you have company in your home and your eye is not always on them, these things can happen. I know you felt secure because he is your boyfriend and maybe you never thought he would do this. But he did do this, and the result from it is devastating.

My motto about snooping is this: I never snoop in other people's stuff because of what I might find. It may be too much for me to handle at the time. I always feel everything will come out in the open sooner or later. And because of the way I think about this, I have never been devastated in this way. But very few people think this way, especially if the opportunity presents itself. Look at it this way; what your boyfriend found out by snooping around has hurt him so deeply that you got him back for that behavior anyway. I hope you get your diary back. And I hope you learn that you really can't trust anyone. I know he regrets the day he went snooping around in your stuff. What he found out was not for him to know, but now he has to live with that nightmare of knowing what he shouldn't know.

If you look at it this way, then maybe you can rest a little easier whether you get your book back or not. But I do hope you get your book back because it is yours. Make peace with the fact that you might not so let it go and move on this time, protecting your things a little better in the future.

444

Situation

98 My Baby's Father's Best Friend

I am dating my baby's father's best friend now. I have admired him ever since I met him. He had a girlfriend, but she was not worthy of him in my opinion.

My man abused me, and I went to his best friend so that he could talk to my man and get him straight. I would cry to him and tell him all of my problems. I started to fall in love with him. He is everything my boyfriend is not. My boyfriend didn't want his baby or me, and his friend was always there for us. It started out as friends.

I don't think my baby's father knows we are involved. It's just that when he finds out, there might be some trouble. Then again if or when he finds out, I don't care if it hurts him or not. He hurt me, so he should get hurt.

Response:

You are dealing with an explosive bomb, it seems to me. This is something that men will want to fight about. If you are dealing with him because you really care, that's one thing. But if this is something you are doing because you are being vengeful, then that's something else. I would think your man's best friend is off limits, just as if he started dating your best friend. I would say expect some problems from this unless this is something the two of them do, date each other's women. The one I am concerned about is the baby. I just hope this does not interfere with the baby's father seeing the baby.

It would have been a bit easier all around if he weren't your man's best friend.

Situation

99 I Am The Cover Girl

That's right, I cover for him. When he wants to impress his friends, he always asks me to escort him somewhere, or sometimes he wants me to give a dinner for his special friends. He loves my home, I live alone, and my home is small, quaint, and quite cute. He says my house reminds him of a doll's house.

Well, since I always pride myself on keeping a beautiful home, this is something I just love doing for him. I just love entertaining, and I can do that every night of the week. That's how I got the name "cover girl" among my friends. I have a little model home, and I definitely don't mind entertaining, so my friends call me the cover girl. When I give a party I get all of my friends together, and we sit around the fireplace and play the piano and sing.

We just have an old-fashioned fun time. I love to cook and bake, and I am good at both. I am a very gracious hostess. This is something I enjoy doing especially for my man. That's right-my man and his special friends. Even though I cover for my man, I know it is something special to him. I am everything his wife is not. I have been there for him when she left him. But he took her back when she came crawling back to him.

I know he'll never be mine, I mean all mine, and because he has always been so good to me, I will always cover for him if he needs me to. The only problem is, will I ever get more than I have now from him? Even though I know he will

never completely be mine, I do want more of him than I have
now. I am just not sure this will ever really happen for us.

Response:

I would like to say you will get more of him eventually,
but I think you know better. He took his wife back after she
left him. I think you already know you have already gotten
the best of the man. You and he have a great relationship the
way it is now. I didn't know he was married. All the times we
talked about him, you never mentioned that he was a married
man.

You really can't demand any more of him because you
know the situation, and you have accepted the situation the
way it is now. I know you want more, but I believe if you
push him for more, you might get less. I really don't understand why you would invest any time or energy in a married
man, period. With a situation like this, there isn't much more
for you to get. I would say, "This, is it." I really don't think
this man will ever leave his wife for anyone.

Situation

100 Should You Pay to Stay

My new boyfriend is wonderful, in so many ways. When it comes to the money thing this is the exception. He is just very money conscious. In a way I admire this but in a way this is a problem for him and now becoming a problem for me.

I just got a promotion on my job so I am making OK money now. I still live at home with my parents and they don't ask for any money from me. My parents want me to take care of myself and save some money for my future. I have been staying at my boyfriend's house a lot. His house really belongs to his parents. They bought a new one and they let him have the one he's in now.

We have been dating for three months now. I moved in with him and recently my boy friend suggested that I pay him a certain amount of rent. Let's just say it's about one-third of my salary. I believe this suggestion came from his parents. My boyfriend said he could give his parents the extra money. He said they would love it. Who wouldn't!

He knows how much I make so what can I really say? I ask a friend of mine what did he think about this and he said to me, "You have to stay somewhere so why not pay him what he wants." I was not too satisfied with that answer since I still can live at my parents' home if I want to. I asked my older sister who is 10 years older than I am, what she thought about it. My sister said, "You should not pay him any money, what if he's using you like a pimp or something." Then she said, "Next he'll be saying give him all your money and he'll buy your clothes."

I'm asking your opinion on this because my sister can be a bit extreme at times. I think she is a little bitter about men anyway. Is she right? What do you think I should do?

Response:

How do you feel about this? There must be some reservation in you if you're asking others for their opinion. I believe things are somewhat new to you right now. You have a new man and a new job promotion. There is a lot to deal with right now.

I can imagine that your feelings are quite busy. You could very well feel overwhelmed now. I would say take it easy right now. I would suggest you stay at home with your parents, and go visit your boyfriend instead of making that your permanent home. There are some real questions you must ask yourself right now. Ask yourself is there any security for you for paying his parents one-third of your monthly salary for staying there. Another question to ask yourself is; what are your boyfriend's intentions for you and him? Does he intend on marrying you in the future or what?

Look at it this way, what if you break up after a year or so? You would have paid $6,000 to $10,000 into a home you now have no claim to. You'll be out of thousands and back at home with your parents. You will lose out in this case. Ask your boyfriend will his parents sell the two of you the home. If he says yes, well at least your making an investment in your future too. If he says no, for some reason then my advice to you is do not do it.

See his parents may feel like three months of knowing someone is not enough time to sell their home to you jointly with their son. In this case I'm sure you can see their point. You should feel after three months of dating a guy why should you start paying him like a renter to stay in his home.

Last but not least look at it another way. This is your man and you are there with him because you are in love with him. Your man wants you to be there because he is in love with you and wants you there with him also. Why then would you pay your boyfriend money to be with him? There are other ways to contribute to the household if you like, contribute money to food, recreation, and things like that. But overall you should save that one-third of your salary a month for yourself in case this relationship does not work out.

Maybe your sister is trying to say to you; if he is supposed to be your man who loves you, then why pay him to stay at his house. If this man really loves you he will encourage your decision to save your money. He should want to show you he has your best interest at heart. He will understand your decision not to pay to stay. Maybe the two of you should be looking to get a place of your own, so that the relationship can have a fresh start.

Situation

101 He's Finally Mine

H e is now a doctor, and a very well known one. I heard he was in town giving a seminar, so I went to see him. I sat in the front row; when he came out, he looked at me, but I was not sure if he recognized who I was.

We have not seen each other for 12 years. At the end of the seminar, I went to him and introduced myself to him, he looked at me and said, "I know, this can't be you!" He grabbed me and hugged me and whispered in my ear, "Are you married?" I was shocked at this question, and I quickly said, "No, I am not."

He wanted me to stay there and wait until he was through so that we could sit and talk. I did and we sat and talked and talked and talked until we had to leave the auditorium. He offered me to go with him to his hotel, but I refused. I told him, "Let's exchange numbers and e-mails," and we did.

That was two weeks ago and everything is still great. It seems as though he and I are finally at the same point in our lives at the same time. I'm still madly in love with him, and he told me he never stop loving me. I think this can work out. The only thing is, I am really getting nervous about everything. It's like I'm getting cold feet or something. Why do you think this is happening to me? This is what I have always wanted.

Response:

The nervousness or fear can be many things. It can be the fear of actually getting what you want. This sounds a bit crazy, but sometimes people get afraid of actually getting what they want. Sometimes we want something so badly that when it seems to be happening, we become afraid of it.

Some people will even sabotage the thing they want out of fear. There also can be some anxiety about getting to know him all over again after 12 years. There may even be some fear of him getting to really know you too. You may be feeling the "what ifs" thing. You know, such as what if this, and what if that. You can be thinking, what if we get to know each other really well, and one or the other or both become disappointed. What if we realize we, are not what each of us want.

I would say to you, Step out on faith instead of fear, and trust that all is going the right way for the two of you now. Remember if the love is there and, has always been there trust in it. Trust that with love, patience, and respect for one another, nothing but the best is in your future. Just breathe through it, one step at a time, and walk into your happiness. Say it's your time to enjoy, and do just that, Enjoy!

Love Letter
Love Is Just Love

Love has nothing to do with anything but itself. Love is just about itself. Love has no care about who you are, when it is in you for someone.

Love has no concern if it is right or wrong. It doesn't care if it should be now or if it should have been then. Love doesn't fight to fit in. Love knows where it is and that it will always be.

Love is never changing. It is a permanent print upon one's heart. See, Love is something unto itself. You can't hide it.
You can't control it and you cannot mold it.

Love sees through circumstances; it understands because it just knows. When you Love someone and you look into the eyes of the one you Love, you will know Love.

Love Is Just Love.

"As I Remain A Woman"

As I remain a woman, I fight this world alone,
Sometimes I roam as a nomad,
With eager fear to go home.

Imagination built my world, Many, many years ago,
But as I seem to twist and toil
There's something I feel I know.

If you can only take my hand, As rough as it may feel
I'll never deny that you're my man,
With faith that I will heal.

I may not make you proud of me, By what I seem to be,
Just hold and kiss and make me free,
So I can be you and you me.

I know you said you have to go, But call me if you can,
I pray someday that you will know,
The woman I really am.

So as I dream my night away, And wake up without
you,
I simply forgot about the day,
My man left me with
Whom?

A feeling trusting human being, Who has seem to lose
her fight,
So still alone I stand to bring,
My love forever in sight.

As I remain a woman, And fight this world alone,
I know it is an Oman,
Why I must fear this home.

Imagination sets me free, With something I've never
known,
So I lie here in this bed,
Paralyzed to my bone.

"The Ocean Deep"

He has a love in his mysterious heart,
He has a vision only,
God can spark.
He has artistry flowing,
To give as his prize.
But he has pain in his eyes.

He has a secret, imbedded within,
He has a sparkle,
Things to bring.
He has an understanding,
Far beyond.
But he has dreams, that are gone.

He has a world, embracing him.
He has a new day,
To conquer.
He has unique philosophies,
To bestow,
But he has so much he's had
To let go.

He has pearls of wisdom,
To give to each,
But more than anything,
He has a love,
That is truly,
The Ocean Deep